MW01537674

LIFE'S
Journey

by Tom Pileggi

GWiz
Publications

Printed in the U.S.A. by

GWiz Publications, Inc.
1111 Easton Road, Suite 27
Warrington, PA 18976

First Printing June 2002 – 5,000 copies
Hardcover: ISBN 0-9717743-0-7
Softcover: ISBN 0-9717743-1-5

Additional copies of *Life's Journey*
can be obtained from:

GWiz Publications, Inc.
1111 Easton Road, Suite 27
Warrington, PA 18976
tel: (215) 343-5130
fax: (215) 343-5106

ISBN 0-9717743-0-7

Preface

I f someone had told me ten years ago that I
would end up in prison, I would have told them
they were crazy. Good guys don't go to prison.
I continue to define myself as a good guy, merely
plagued by a bad situation.

As the eighth of nine children, I have succeeded
professionally and personally through the traditional
values instilled by my father: working hard, earning
respect, and maintaining integrity. My father insisted
upon these values for the preservation of a reputable
name, a name earned through my career as builder,
developer, and financier. This name secured my position
as a board member at Cheltenham Bank, a community
bank with which I have done business since the age of
six. Uncovering and reporting an eighty-five million
dollar loss fueled my personal battle to save the bank
from oblivion. That battle was lost, along with the bank,
and the two hundred and sixty jobs that came with it.

Shortly after, the Mayor of Philadelphia solicited
my services in establishing the largest charitable organization in the history of the city. Through no fault of
my own, I was again forced into defeat, learning that
the best intentions can produce the most unexpected

consequences. Somewhere down the line, the partici-
pants and the events of the bank and the charity became
intertwined, resulting in my unjust conviction on insider
trading and nineteen months imprisonment.

Only four months after my release, I sit at my desk
at First Cheltenham Financial Corporation; a mortgage
company founded by me with the hopes of one day
reestablishing the lost Cheltenham Bank. The office is
quieter than before, offering solace to a rapidly aging
man. I have returned to my previous life with optimism
for the future. Yet, I cannot ignore the gray hairs that
record the years, or the confirmation of experience so
deeply written in the wrinkles across my brow.

At fifty-six years old, the past looms upon me
through the haze of memory, dimmed within prison
walls. Before the past is lost to my present situation,
I begin a new battle. I begin a literary battle in an attempt to clear my name.

With great effort, I recall the carefree roam of life,
when no thought of shadows disrupted my path. More
vividly, I account the train of circumstances that led to
my conviction. For my own consideration as well as for
the reader's, I restrict myself to the inner life of a particular man, and the external events that clouded an
individual career.

I write this autobiography, sacrificing my memories to the written word, in an effort to gain an understanding ear. I write this autobiography for my family
and all the employees at Cheltenham Bank, so that they
will understand how a good guy goes to prison.

Table of Contents

Dedicated to my grandchildren
Krista, Erika, Jenna, and Tommy,
and to all of the fine employees who lost their jobs at
Cheltenham Bank.

And to the two women that held my heart, Josephine
and Mildred. May they rest in peace.

All proceeds from this book will be donated to
**The Children's Hospital of Philadelphia
and Abington Memorial Hospital.**

Special thanks to:

Diane and Terry, for all your help
in the completion of this book.
Here's to us and the unexpected paths in life!

Liz, for the faith, and the understanding!

Dr. Ruth Westrick, for believing in me, and
Chief Johnson and his family, for the friendship.

"A successful person is one who can lay a firm foundation with the bricks that others throw at him or her."   *—David Brinkley*

Chapter 1

THE GARDENER'S BOY

My father rode a big fish from the small town
of Maida, Italy, to America, bringing only his
talking dog, "Baruno," to direct the fish safely.
Throughout the years, he elaborated on this story
nightly as he tucked his nine children into bed.

Reaching adulthood, we realized that his emigra-
tion was a traditional one, leaving his uncharted mountain town for the prosperity offered in the United States.
My father's freight ship reached its New York port in
the early 1920's, after he had left his entire family behind in search of a better opportunity.

At the age of eighteen, my father, Bruno Pileggi,
found that opportunity in the form of landscaping. He
quickly found a home in Elkins Park, Pennsylvania, on
the family estate of George Elkins, industrialist and
entrepreneur. My father resided in a row of cramped employee housing, while earning his keep as caretaker and
master gardener of the elaborate grounds.

Four years later, after an introduction by a mutual friend, my father met and married Mary Grispino, whose family had emigrated from Italy a generation before. The estate had passed from Elkins to Stephano, yet my parents remained for eighteen years, raising seven of their nine children in the two bedrooms of the gardener's quarters. It was not until the age of forty that my father began his own landscaping business, leaving the Stephano estate behind for a more independent career with builder, A.P. Orleans.

A.P. Orleans supplied my father with our first house, located on the corner of Ashbourne and Spring Avenues. In exchange for the home and minimal income, my father cared for the acres of estate grounds, now home to Lynnewood Gardens. The recently condemned three bedroom home had been artistically constructed of granite stone with arched windows, a cedar shake

Bruno and Mary Pileggi

roof, and a flat-topped wooden vestibule, supported by striking pillars, over the doorway. The home marked the entrance of the Orleans estate, while the opportunity marked my father's start in landscape design.

The extra bedroom allowed for extra children, regardless of continued financial struggles. I was the first addition to the new home. My mother gave birth to me, in Temple University Hospital, on May 10, 1945. The hospital released my mother, and her newly named son, Thomas, to my father days later. Unable to pay for the medical services rendered, my father was required to leave his watch as collateral. In the future, he would joke that he should have kept the watch and left the son.

Three years after my birth, my mother delivered her final child, concluding with nine: Frankie, John, Rosemary, Maryann, Ann, Vince, Joe, Tommy, and Margie. Twelve months later, in search of a larger house, my father exhausted his savings by purchasing a tiny four bedroom Victorian on Spring Avenue. The home's wooded Dutch lap siding and slated roof stood modestly among the prosperity of surrounding German styled stone homes. Located within walking distance from the Orleans estate, my father continued his employment while giving birth to his own nursery on the acre of land directly behind our home.

Spring Avenue houses my strongest and fondest reminiscences of youth. It is from there that the gray ruins of memory are startled into a thousand recollections of the former and simpler sphere of life. I still remember the pleasures that came with ice cream on every third week, or with the public pool twice a summer. I remember the anticipation of eleven birthday cakes a year and Sunday brunch weekly. I easily recall the tranquility in my mother's face as she crocheted, and in my father's as he sipped Italian wine on the front porch. I recall the pride felt in my father's ability to

The author's childhood home on Spring Avenue

earn a dollar and in my mother's ability to stretch it. Above all, I recollect the general freedom of childhood spirit and the daily carelessness that came with it.

Evenings began with the roar of the 55 Bus, halting at the corner to release my older siblings from a hard day's work. I would abandon my elaborate forts and tunnels built in neighboring woods, to run and meet my oldest brother, Frankie. We would share the walk home, following the intoxicating aroma of my mother's fresh baked apple and cherry pies, originating from the fruits of my father's nursery. Close to supper, the nine children would gather on the wraparound porch, waiting for the silence that came with a dish of macaroni, a homemade pizza or a handrolled gnocchi.

After dinner, my father would interrupt my return to the woods, sending his "little builder" around the corner to Farber's Drug Store for his small tipped cigars. Reluctantly, I would leave alone, only to hear Frankie's heavy steps catching up from behind. Frankie liked being the oldest and he took the responsibility seriously.

Often, he would accompany me, postponing the errand for the sake of childlike adventure.

Frankie and I frequently returned home to the echo of my mother's sweet hum as my father played beautiful music on his harmonica. We silently bickered for our turn on the retiring porch swing as we followed my father's gaze to the delicate appeal of my mother in the dimmed porch light. Her amber tinted curls fell unbound around her face, highlighting flawless features upon fair skin. My father's distinction bore a more rugged appeal of chiseled olive beneath a heavy head of side-slicked darkness. I remember the mild scent of Ivory soap clinging to my father's fresh washed skin, as he leaned over our beds nightly. Prepared with an old Italian fable, or a tale of his rustic hometown left behind, my father remained faithful to the tradition of storytelling, emphasizing the distinct lessons each story had to offer.

Of my father's lessons, he maintained that it is not what you make, but what you save that counts. Surrounded by educated wealth, I learned to listen well and pay no mind to the childhood teasing for the patches on my pants. My father worked hard for what little we had and was well respected among the adult members of the community. I was proud to be called the "gardener's boy."

Everyday, my father left for work before we woke up for school and returned just before dark for my mother to peel the sweat-

The author on the day of his first Holy Communion, May 18, 1952.

stained T-shirt off his sun-glazed body. It was this example of hard work that encouraged my own business start at the age of six.

I began modestly by mowing lawns during the summer. Within the year, I was shoveling snow in the winter, selling newspapers around town, shining shoes in the barbershop, playing stock boy and soda jerk at Mayfair's Drug Store, and cleaning under the bleachers after ball games at Cheltenham High School. I developed a five-year plan for business and financial quotas, depositing three dollars weekly into a savings account at the local Cheltenham Bank. My father's face glowed, reflecting my own pride, when I showed him the first pair of shoes that I had purchased with my own money. My mother used to joke, "My baby is a man at six years old." She was right.

As a boy, I learned lessons generally reserved for men. Mr. Finkel, a local clothing storeowner, taught me early about the shrewdness in choosing clients. Equipped with only a shovel and a pair of socks on my hands, I persevered for three hours to complete a three-dollar job. After shoveling and cleaning his entire driveway, Finkel refused to pay.

When I returned home, I called Chief Johnson of Cheltenham police. Chief Johnson, an acquaintance and customer from the barbershop, sympathized, instructing me to shovel the snow back onto Finkel's drive. When detected, Mr. Finkel approached me with language inappropriate for my youthful ear. As I lost my nerve, I gained an ally in the Cheltenham squad car that arrived. The officer made Finkel pay and insisted that I leave the snow.

Mr. Diamond of Diamond's Food Market intended a similar lesson, and in the process, taught me more than he realized. He purchased the empty soda bottles that I received in exchange for cleaning the high school bleachers. Coca Cola bottles sold for two cents and the Ginger Ale bottles sold for five, under Mr. Diamond's insistence that I wash and rack them myself. He demanded ten free bottles per bulk sale, saying that he was teaching me a lesson that I would not understand until older. I understood it earlier than he anticipated, taking ten bottles off the rack each time and bringing them back for resale. I ran into Mr. Diamond when I was sixteen and at the start of my building career. He finally revealed his "secret" lesson, which was not to let anyone take advantage of me. I revealed my own secret that he had not.

Shining shoes at the barbershop in Elkins Park Square demonstrated the more costly lesson of respecting yourself and the service that you provide. A wealthy elderly man fond of cigars had become a repeat client at my shoeshine. As I would shine, he would ash his cigar on my head, amusing only himself. I found it worth the ten-cent tip, allowing the habitual behavior to continue. On one occasion, his amusement set my hair on fire. Causing more fear than damage, the gentleman dismissed the incident with the flip of a quarter, adding, "As long as you shine shoes, Kid, I'm going to have a little fun with you." I polished not only his shoes that day, but also his socks and pant leg. The elderly man's objection rang throughout the barbershop, as I flipped back his quarter. The cigar smoker was forbidden back in the shop and I forbid myself to ever be bought. Now, I realize that these lessons learned so early in life would be repeated in my future, with consequences much more severe.

While learning the lessons of an entrepreneur, I attended school on the side, maintaining good grades with little effort at Saint James Parochial. Saint James was a small parish, combining a small church and small school in a Gothic styled stone building. The church rested on the bottom floor, supporting two floors of overcrowded classrooms above. In my spare time, I was an altar boy and sang baritone in the church choir. These two activities earned me the nuns' affection and, eventually, the honorable role of "Pope" in the May Procession. But, by the age of eight, the lure of sports led me from the choir to the football field.

Despite being the smallest player on the team, I earned the position of second string, never fearing the bigger guys. I allowed the force of my entire body to back each collision. This force and fearlessness merited

Saint James Parish and School

the short-lived position of quarterback. With hands too small to hold onto the ball, my versatility was challenged again in the position of half back. My brother Frankie began to coach me, after I moved from Saint James to the Willow Grove Boys Club, a club founded by him and my cousin Mick. Football continued till the age of fourteen, when my career came to a halt with my height. Now, at fifty-six years old, I remain a steady five foot and six inches; yet, the fearlessness and force has remained.

At the same time I entered the football field, I entered a new field in business. My father handed me a pick and shovel, soliciting me for the family trade. He told me to start digging and confirmed that the time had come to "go to hard work." Unwilling to sacrifice my profitable odd jobs, I had little time for the intensity of manual labor. I accepted the pick and shovel, but not without noticing the printed name of J.J. Shanigan's Hardware Store on their handles. My father had intended for me to use the tools, instead I sold them, along with many others. I bought from J.J. Shanigan's at wholesale and resold them at retail in a local gas station. I supplied the station's owner with fifty-cents per tool for rent of the space, and maintained fifty to seventy-five cents each as profit.

With retail sales as my most profitable business, I began to spend less time on my education. The teachers became aware of my extra curricular activities, as I frequently began cutting classes. At the time, I felt they were teaching what I already knew. Although the nuns had encouraged my increasing odd jobs around the building, they begged me to slow down outside of school. In a family of eleven, I was only doing my fair share, contributing to the household while starting a savings of my own. The teachers disagreed and kept me in detention regularly, so that I "could rest." In an attempt to deter the more frequent incidents of escaping, they would keep my jacket locked away. The brutal winter months taught me to leave a plastic-wrapped jacket in the nearby bushes. My escape through the window to the jacket waiting below became a laughing matter; yet, they never stopped trying.

I felt that my youth had passed by the age of nine, when my mother suffered a stroke. The family's eagerness of hope subsided to the apathy of despair, as my mother suffered three progressive strokes the same year, paralyzing the right side of her brain. The woman, who had cradled me with loving conversation, rested immobile and nonresponsive, with a newly dulled spirit reflected through hollow eyes. My mother's disability was the first real pain of my life, overburdening me with a sickness in my heart. I responded by initializing a pattern of comfort found in the isolation of business. Hefty hospital bills increased the need for family income and encouraged my emotional escape into the methodical world of work. My family learned quickly that life rejected heartache and proceeded, as did we. The older girls resumed household duties, while we all shared the responsibility of my mother's home care for years to come.

The difficulty of home care intensified with my mother's waning condition. Eventually, she was moved to Homestead Convalescent in Willow Grove, where she remained for thirty years. My father moved the entire family to a tiny split level in Glenside, which gave my father the opportunity and the convenience to feed my mother three times daily. Years later, with his children grown, my father would take an apartment within walking distance of the Homestead. His devotion to my mother would remain until his own death at eighty-two years old. At a meager eighty-five pounds, while supporting the heart of an ox, my mother would follow him, only five years later.

When my father first moved us to the new home, he established an independent nursery on a nearby plot of land. All of the Pileggi boys were required to work in that nursery, as an answer to the increased financial burdens of my mother's illness. My father's business examples illustrated the values found at home. He worked hard with integrity and respect, and never tired in providing for his family. My work in the nursery taught me the value of a handshake and the value of a dollar. I proceeded with many odd jobs on the side including a brief career of buying, restoring, and selling cars.

After I completed the ninth grade in Abington Junior High School, the teachers at Saint James received notice of their defeat. Despite their past objections, I followed the example set by my brothers and dropped out of high school at sixteen to work full time. When I quit school, Johnny and Vince were already well settled in the family trade. I helped in the nursery as long as I could, but failed to recognize a future. I longed for something more, to establish a business and a reputable name of my own. Deserting all other side jobs, I taught myself the building business and the financial aspects related.

With ten thousand dollars saved, Cheltenham Bank took a chance and matched my savings with a loan. I purchased a rundown property on Apsley Street in Germantown and renovated the home into four apartments. The continual purchase, rehabilitation, and resale of several homes established my modest track record in the business. In spite of tough times, I pursued my goals with perseverance and dedication. At the age of eighteen, I took my first plunge in new construction, after generating enough revenue to purchase my first piece of land in the then undeveloped and inexpensive Doylestown Township.

The opportunities were there and the time was right. A bit of luck and a ton of hard work dictated the immediate launch of my building career. My preferences for stone, white brick, and stucco differentiated the exterior of my homes from the rest. I believed in variety of style and characterized each home beyond its typecast name. Before long, I succeeded as a builder and financier. With my reputation established, I took a chance in cluster housing by building affordable homes in wide-open spaces. This chance soon became my signature, opening the door to tudor-style developments that would predominate in the future. After taking a chance with my career, I decided to seize an opportunity in my personal life and steered toward the next step in my current five-year plan.

Chapter 2

THE RAVEN AND
THE DOVE

Since the age of thirteen, I had spared enough time to fall in love with and court a dark Italian beauty. Maria was the daughter of Santoro, my father's closest friend and "piazon." Raised in the same hometown in Italy and immigrating only years apart, Santoro and my father were like brothers. Maria and I had been reared closely, encouraged in our early years toward an adolescent match. Movies, dances, and family functions had led to our youthful engagement, validating the expectations of both families. Maria and I shared laughter at the seemingly traditional arranged marriage as we began to plan for the future.

Throughout our engagement, I continued with my commitment to building, rationalizing it as a commitment to the family that I hoped to soon have. For that family, I strived seven days and nights weekly, securing the immediate success of my business. I was spending less time with Maria and more time on the job site, until just before our intended September wedding when I had completed building and furnishing our future home.

My future became unsettled through reported rumors from a loyal friend only two weeks before the wedding. My own ache mirrored in his stammering voice as he revealed Maria's relationship with a man twenty years her senior, a married Montgomery County police officer. I listened to his words, but absorbed only the infidelities of Maria's masked virtue and masked sentiment. That evening, I picked up Maria to select our silver set as planned. Throughout the night, she had complained of a headache before asking to be delivered home for an early night's sleep. I dropped her off and, at the risk of shaming myself, parked around the corner and waited. After forty-five minutes of vacant staring, I started my car to leave, dismissing my friend's previous report. I found my optimism premature, when I witnessed Maria hurry from the house to an unfamiliar car in the driveway.

The car led me into Northeast Philadelphia and down Roosevelt Boulevard to the Blue Light Cabins, an inexpensive motel suiting the occasion. I remained in the parking lot long enough to confirm the couple checking in. After hours of aimless driving, I returned home to increasing restlessness. I cancelled the wedding the following day, preserving Maria's feigned virtue with a lack of explanation. Her reaction told me that she knew. She carefully chose her questions, fearing the honest answers that I could never divulge.

Our two families pursued the breakup more harshly, demanding explanations to their disappointments. Their ceaseless questions encouraged a two-week escape to Florida. My brother Frankie offered his silent support by driving me to the airport with no questions asked. In honor of my requests, he erased all evidence of Maria before my return. Frankie sold the furnished house, returned the already accepted gifts, and settled any remaining discrepancies. When I arrived home, I needed only to recuperate my heartache in the distractions of work. Maria's memory soon faded, despite the weight of family resentment that would remain for years to come.

Twelve years later, Maria would walk unannounced into my Glenside office with her third husband, both looking for work and a place to live. I housed them rent-free in one of my forty-eight unit developments, appointing her husband Superintendent while Maria collected rent. They did well, but I stayed away, sending my foreman to represent me when an appearance was needed. A couple years after they began employment, Maria divorced the third and married a fourth husband. She remained in the development that, at the time, I was preparing to sell. I offered Maria a final favor and sold her the house at cost. I saw her rarely after that, although she continued casual correspondence through birthday and holiday cards.

With Maria's fourth marriage, my father accepted a long denied realization. "Four husbands in so few years?" he asked. "We're not stupid, Tommy." Despite my father's leading question, I remained faithful to Maria, never revealing that evening at Blue Light Cabins. He pushed the issue slightly, until I reminded him of his four grandchildren and my lovely wife waiting at home. I had left Maria behind a long time ago, while my father and Santoro had passed silent blame for the failed relationship. At last, he too put Maria in the past, and placing his hand on my shoulder, offered a voiceless comfort intended for the years before.

I met my lovely wife when I was nineteen, while still followed by the shadow of Maria. The immediate growth of my building career had publicly defined me a financial success. However, my own definition of success included a family. I found my willing partner for that family in Elizabeth Provasnik, an Austrian immigrant only four months younger than myself.

My first meeting with Liz was at a German Hungarian Club in Philadelphia, which she frequented with her family. She earned my attention with her dynamic spirit and wholesome smile, a smile that held the warmth of the sun's rays. Too shy to ask her to dance, I had sent a friend to orchestrate an introduction. The pure brilliance of her blue eyes, blonde hair and fair skin lustered over the memory of Maria's dark seduction. Three months into our dating, I casually proposed, after warning Liz of my endless hours at work. She broke off a long engagement to a composer, who still lived in Austria. Within the year we were married, agreeing to a small, traditional Italian wedding.

Despite Liz's beauty, I had approached our marriage systematically, as I had begun to do all things in life. Avoiding the risks of vulnerability, I fought the complexities of love and instead married on the basis of respect. I respected Liz and the decency instilled from her family. As a churchgoing Christian, she exemplified the values associated with a charitable heart. She was a good woman from good stock. At the time, that was enough.

Over time, my feelings for Liz evolved, rendering her the second and final love of my life. Age produced an increased understanding and the recognition of a love that continues to grow thirty-six years later. We have argued through imperfect times, but our marriage has persisted through traditional values from generations past. Through hard work, we modestly raised four children, encouraging the formal education we lacked. Mutual respect for our opposing natures has offered the patience to accept what we do not necessarily comprehend. And above all, integrity with ourselves and with each other has furnished the security of a shared future.

Today, I continue to view Liz as the angelic woman that I first perceived her to be. Her smile is as contagious as her heart, both large enough to encompass the universe. With our children grown, Liz fills her time feeding the homeless at St. Francis's soup kitchen in Kensington and making rosary beads with her church group. She volunteers both time and money to our shared charities while adding to her list of sponsored children in India. Perhaps, I did not fully realize both the physical and the spiritual beauty of Liz upon our first meeting, but I certainly realize it now. If her flight to Heaven is not secured in her heartfelt deeds, it is secured in the thirty-six years of putting up with me.

When first married, Liz's patience had been tested time and again. She withstood my sleepless nights and unorthodox hours. Her marriage to a workaholic presented many challenges, beginning with our living arrangements. Sample homes for each new development repeatedly provided temporary residence. I converted each garage into an office for the proximity to both the work site and my children. By the time Liz was pregnant with our fourth child, she had already suffered through six moves in eight years. At the age of twenty-six, when our most recent residence sold, I finally decided on settling down.

Equipped with only a handful of laborers and a mental image, our dream home was realized in only three months. From the exterior, the home is rather large, but simple, most closely resembling a colonial-style home, constructed of white brick. Remembering my first childhood home with A.P. Orleans, I included a large vestibule in front with striking pillars, which supported its peaked roof. Beneath it was another smaller vestibule, with similar pillars, which supports a balcony entered from the second floor hallway, and covers the home's gold wrought iron-gated doorway. The doorway is guarded by the marbled eyes of gold-laced concrete lions, standing tall on opposite sides of the pillars. I have been told that the pillars offer a southern gentility to the home, in the tradition of a Virginia plantation.

Perhaps overdeveloped at the time, the two-story, five-bedroom home now compares favorably to some of the newer developments. Although partially concealed within a three-foot stone wall, a circular brick driveway joins its open-gated entrance and exit. The home has served as a model for local builders, attempting, but never succeeding, at its exact duplication.

Located across the street from a golf course and behind a bird sanctuary, the home continues as a sanctuary of my own, offering the earned serenity of a raised family and a retired building career. Memories of my own children are refreshed in the lighthearted play of my grandchildren throughout the increasingly adorned lawns. I now manicure my lawns into gardens as a gift to them, a wonderland fruiting from their grandfather's labor. I treasure this time with my grandchildren in an attempt to recapture the days lost, when building had won over their parents.

Chapter 3

THE BULL, THE BUM, AND FLIP

My enthusiasm for building could not be denied. It swelled since my youth and reached its summit in my adult life. The building business offered pleasures beyond those expected of a career. It became a hobby and my most preferred pastime.

I found fulfillment in the development of each home, similar to my father's fulfillment found in trees. Both of us realized dreams through the use of our hands. He grazed in the dirt to plant seeds, and I grazed in concrete to lay foundations. With careful labor and attention, we both nurtured our projects through their growth, until one day they would reach full bloom. I witnessed my father's disappointment over the years, as he handed over a prized tree for the paling pleasure of profit. I felt that same disappointment with the sale of each home.

When I began building in Doylestown, I willingly invested infinite time and tireless energy. Most months were spent residing in sample homes. It offered my accessibility as project manager, and allowed me to remain manually active on each site. At the same time, the sample homes supplied the office space needed for book-keeping, sales, and advertising, all of which I did on my own. My increasing responsibilities as sole proprietor of the business necessitated the hand picking of reliable employees. The best of them were irreplaceable, and remained as friends until their death.

"Kelly the Bum" was the first laborer selected. I suppose he was also the most unusual, since I found him on the streets of Cheltenham. I had known Kelly since my youth. For as long as I could remember, Kelly lived in abandoned cars behind the gas station, sweeping local bars for free drinks. He was spare and tall, hiding his height in a permanent slouch. Beneath his weather-rouged cheeks, brunette whiskers matched his matted hair that had grown unheeded, floating about the face. He was well known in the area and protected as part of the community. On winter nights, Cheltenham Police took Kelly to the county jail for odd jobs and a warm place to sleep. During the day, Kelly would stop me on my route to school. With an Irish brogue revealing an earlier immigration, he would ask, "Young fellow, got any loose change for ole' Kelly?"

His red nose, liquor-laced breath, and sharp stench revealed his problem with alcohol. I often flipped him the change, but required a promise that I knew would be broken. I asked him to promise that the money never be spent on liquor. I had no doubt that it was, after witnessing his condition on my return from school. As a child, I had allowed Kelly to sell newspapers with me, giving him his share of profit. As an adult, I took Kelly off the streets to Bucks County where we found his talent as a valued and gifted painter.

With Kelly's new career came his sobriety. Food replaced alcohol, and Kelly gained fifteen pounds to his one hundred and thirty-pound frame. His newly washed and rubberbanded hair complimented his new clothing, offering an overall healthier appearance. I supplied Kelly with temporary housing in sample homes, until his savings earned him a Cheltenham home of his own. It was not until later in life that Kelly revealed his story. Many years earlier, a drinking and driving accident, with Kelly at the wheel, had killed his wife. Self-blame and depression had taken him deeper into alcohol dependency, eventually leading to his life on the streets. Kelly continued to paint for me until close to his death at eighty years old. All the while, he remained a sober bachelor. My experience with "Kelly the Bum" taught me that success is irrelevant to money.

Shortly after hiring Kelly, my early fondness of stone fronts led me to a bull. On a daily basis, I admired the anonymous work of Tony Delciotto at a local WaWa in the process of construction. One afternoon in passing, I caught the artist still at work. Driving a company truck loaded with windows, I slammed on the breaks, losing half of my cargo, but gaining a valued friend. I wasted little time with introductions and solicited his services as stonemason. In a heavy Italian accent, he said, "You're kidding. You want me to work for a kid like you?" Tony Delciotto did and continued to call me "Sonny Boy" until his death, over twenty years after our first meeting.

Tony was a bull with a heavy handshake. His five-foot-four-inch frame supported arms and legs of steel, contrasting the distinguished charm of his frequently smoked pipe. Although rough in size and manner, Tony was blessed with noble good looks. Silken threads of gray clustered over his brow, capping a chiseled face with a finely molded protruding chin. His tanned complexion pulled tight around the eyes, emphasizing a hard darkness. While his features offered a trace of regality, his eyes portrayed a man not to be reckoned with.

When Tony was seventy-four years old, a rare occasion called for his demonstration of strength while working at one of my developments. After a practical joke was played in poor taste, Tony mechanically rose in retaliation. He calmly picked up the culprit, and threw the coworker through a bay window. The victim was five feet, ten inches tall and beefy enough to walk away with only a bruised body that matched his bruised pride. The coworker excused the punishment, as a result of his own stupidity. He messed with the bull and got the horns.

I heard of the incident and the broken window from my foreman, yet I insisted on paying Tony in full, at week's end. Tony would not hear of it and threatened to quit if a three-hundred-dollar deduction was not made for the price of the window. Tony was perhaps the only man as stubborn as I. Consequently, he got his way. If Tony's great principle and pride were not easily detected by his behavior, they were certainly detected in his handshake.

Tony was a man of honor, faithful in word and thought. He was the type of man to always look you firmly in the eye. We had mutual respect for each other and our opinions. Both being men of our word, we never shared a contract beyond the shake of a hand. We often pingponged professional ideas off each other and ended up learning personal lessons that placed our friendship outside the borders of business.

Tony carried on the work of ten men until his lung cancer was diagnosed in 1990. He refused medical treatment for the cancer and retired to his room for the ten-month duration of his illness. At eighty-four years old, Tony held firmly to his image of strength, despite his fading condition. Since he refused to be seen by anyone except his wife, visiting was through locked doors. Until his death, Tony joked through a closed door during my frequent hour-long visits, never hinting to the pained skeleton he had become. He will forever, in my eyes, remain the bull with the heavy handshake. The quality and character of his work continues to be admired anonymously in the homes that remain today.

Quality, integrity, and keeping my word had always marked the character of my business and I increasingly relied on the power of a handshake. The success of the business developed with my love. I loved what I was doing and my reward was doing it well. Consequently, I had acquired some degree of wealth along the way. I would be lying to say that I did not enjoy it. I was easily able to offer my family comforts that my parents had been unable to provide.

However, my modest roots as a Cheltenham boy cautioned me against frivolous and careless spending. I believed in sharing profits with those who helped me earn them, and those who most desperately needed them. I had established ongoing bonus opportunities for my employees who successfully met deadlines. I also donated a percentage of each home to growing charities. The money left over was spent or invested with a clear conscience.

Like many, I could have given in to the wealth, but I worked hard to remain unaffected. I had always been, and will always be, "Tommy" Pileggi, the guy who eternally wears dungarees, sneakers, and a T-shirt, both in the office and out. I forbade money to serve as my God and refused to be defined by the dollar.

I defined my business success through the number of houses built, the number of my images turned into reality. At twenty-one years old, I had succeeded with fifty-five homes built. At twenty-five, three hundred homes confirmed my success, as I continued to work seven days and nights with no shame in manual labor. By the age of twenty-nine, with my housing success more than doubled, I had begun to expand into shopping centers and industrial buildings. It was at twenty-nine that I suffered my first heart attack.

At the time, I had seventeen projects in the making and was building in Bucks and Montgomery counties, as well as Philadelphia and New Jersey. The nuns of my youth echoed in my father's voice as he warned me to slow down. From experience, he had told me that I could not continue at the same pace. I was headed for a crash. I ignored his warning, maintaining the same intensity that turned childhood odd jobs into a multimillion dollar business. Three weeks after my father had spoken his words, I collapsed on the job site, while pouring concrete in a hundred and four degrees temperature.

The mild heart attack was obvious, but the diagnosis of hypertension and premature arthritis that had accompanied took some time to confirm. In addition, the doctors offered the first identification of a lifelong anxiety disorder, explaining my "why put off till tomorrow, what you can do today" mentality. Four weeks in a hospital bed prescribed not only a number of medications, but also an amendment in my current five-year plan. I committed myself to a new work ethic, 90% brainpower and 10% manual labor, replacing the previous 50/50 balance. I took the hint the heart attack had to offer and revised my one-man army into an organization.

For the first time in my career, a secretary was hired. Frankie, who had been encouraging me to slow down all the while, introduced me to his childhood friend, Helen Wahl. She was hired as my secretary on his word alone. I could have never anticipated her competence or loyalty. Helen had a cheerful nature that could sugar anything sour. With uncomplaining compliance, she organized both the office and my life on a regular basis. Helen worked with me tirelessly for over twenty years, before retiring in one of my nearby developments. Today, I wonder if the business could have ever survived without her.

Shortly after hiring Helen, I went in search of a foreman. On a fellow builder's suggestion and reference, one was hired. With the new addition to the business, I looked forward to finding a trace of leisure in my life. I relied on him as a competent worker and a good man, able to oversee construction in my absence. I never counted on his questionable integrity that, unfortunately, had taken me a few years to realize.

Three years after my foreman had first been employed, one of my contractors came to me with a complaint. My foreman had been requiring financial kickbacks from several of the contractors. It had been going on for quite some time, before it was brought to my attention. As my direct representative, the foreman was jeopardizing my name and reputation, as well as the success of my business. However, I was not prepared to take steps against him without proof. After writing down the serial numbers of several fifty-dollar bills, I gave the contractor this money to pay off the foreman.

Anthony DelCiotto and Dan Filipone

The same day the contractor handed the money over, I called the foreman to my office. After casual business conversation, I dismissed him, saying that I was headed to buy a card for my Godchild's birthday. I put on a show, checking my wallet for her gift. I pulled out several twenty-dollar bills and asked if he had any big bills in place of my smaller ones. The foreman offered me two fifties and I made the exchange without any question.

After he left my office, I checked the serial numbers, confirming a match to the ones noted previously. I knew I was in a jam. If I fired him immediately, I would be left without a foreman, a necessity in my growing business. I decided to sit on the situation until finding an appropriate replacement.

That replacement was Danny Filipone; Flip as he became known, after being nicknamed by Tony. I had known Danny since I was a kid, when, as a sixteen year old boy, he had worked for A.P. Orleans with several other members of his family. His family stayed with A.P. Orleans, while Danny found employment with a larger company in 1969. I remembered his work quality well, along with his determined and indefatigable spirit. It was eight years after he left Orleans, and I was dogged in hunting him down. I called Booie Flitter, the nephew of Orleans, who still had contact with Danny's family. At a mutual friend's wedding, Booie ran into Danny's cousin Frank, telling him to have Danny give me a call.

On July 7, 1977, Danny came to work for me as foreman, after I tactfully allowed his predecessor to resign. Danny was only slightly taller than myself and in exceptional form. His body was athletically lean, detailing curves of physical strength. His happy-go-lucky air often revealed too freely his sympathetic heart. But, a boisterous tone and vein of dry humor had won the respect of the men.

It was no coincidence when practical jokes and laughter followed Danny to each job site. Nonetheless, he was a hard worker with high standards, demanding results that satisfied his perfectionist nature. He has never given me a reason to doubt my confidence in his discretion or fidelity. As an honest and reliable man, Danny held a similar work ethic as my own, and burned the candle from both ends. It took its toll many years later, when he was hospitalized for a triple bypass in 1998. He took only ten days off before returning to the office.

Today, Danny continues to work for me, confined to the office with a decreased workload. Closing in on retirement, I joke that he cannot leave the business until I do. He still regularly visits my home in the early morning before going to the office, as he had done so many years in the past. Over our twenty-five years together, Danny has become one of my closest friends and confidantes. By all means, he is family, earning the affection generally reserved for brothers.

Danny "Flip" Filipone

Chapter 4

FRANKIE

Frankie was my father's oldest son and I the youngest. Throughout our lives, we were the closest, sharing our time and interests. Frankie was the first to find a career outside of my father's nursery, when he began a profitable life in pharmaceutical sales. Years later, he dismissed profit for pleasure, adventuring into an insurance business of his own. With his new career came our bartering of services. Insurance policies were traded for buildings, dismissing the need to ever exchange a dollar. I remained faithful to my pleasures of building; yet took notice of the success Frankie found in life's varied challenges.

With a head of unbound midnight curls and liquid green eyes, Frankie resembled Tony Bennett. Rather, as Frankie would say, Tony Bennett looked like him. His large teasing smile and slightly protruding tongue, escaped scarlet plush lips, manifesting a dimple-laced face and an enchantment for life. Frankie's voice had a whimsical chime that appeared to reflect the innermost man. He gave that inner man freely to the world, never hiding in self-consciousness.

Everyday was Christmas with Frankie. The bonfire in his heart warmed the rose tan of his cheeks. His vigor was nature's gift, spreading the holiday joy daily, while masking his bear-like physique beneath a jolly demeanor. His brawn was illustrated only in swallowing hugs offered freely to those around him. Frankie's physical strength could allow him to carry a filing cabinet across his chest and down a flight of stairs, but it paled in comparison to his mental strength. As a motivator, he unrolled his positive attitude toward anyone that crossed his path, offering endless verbal support and encouraging the full development of individual potential. Frankie listened to people, believing in who they were and what they had to say. Most of all, he believed in himself and the power of the human spirit.

Frankie had a heart problem of his own, and tried to teach me to relax, bringing me to the ball games he would coach or to the parks where he spent his time and money. He continuously encouraged me to diversify my experience by finding a hobby outside of business. Frankie knew how to live and often got on me to do the same.

I found my own richness in life when sharing Frankie's company. His love for food took us on long drives in search of fresh fish and produce markets. Our wives joked of our boyish manners, as we'd run around town, leaving the mark of laughter at every stop. Sometimes we would just do nothing, enjoying only our conversations traced with the dryness of shared humor. I valued all my time spent with Frankie. He took not only the responsibility of big brother, but also that of best friend.

I kept Frankie's advice for a hobby in mind while attending a Las Vegas building convention at the start of 1977. The final night of the convention, I caught stand-up comedian, Joan Rivers, at the MGM Grande.

Her comical style never earned the laughter that I reserved for the likes of Jimmy Durante, however, I found humor in the concept of her upcoming film, *Rabbit Test*. The film, co-written by Joan, was a comedy about the first pregnant man. It would be Joan's directorial debut. My curiosity increased as she turned her routine into a solicitation for investors. I scribbled my name, number, and interest on a napkin, remembering an earlier promise to get Frankie to Hollywood one day. With previous investments in only real estate and the stock market, I laughed at the idea of a Hollywood hobby. I left Las Vegas the following day and returned home in anticipation of an upcoming family vacation.

For several months, the Pileggi men had been planning a Florida vacation. It was to be my father's first plane ride and an overdue reunion for his five boys. I returned from Vegas on a Wednesday and spent the majority of the night at Frankie's, making up for time missed while away. The next day, my father and Frankie were the first to depart for Miami Beach. I stayed behind to finish up business from the convention and agreed to meet them the Saturday that followed. My other three brothers would join us the next week.

Thursday, at three in the afternoon, my father called my Glenside office to inform me of their safe arrival at the Holiday Inn on Collins Avenue. An hour and a half later, as I was continuing with business, my father called again. Frankie had suffered a massive heart attack and fell dead on the hotel floor. He was forty-nine years old. There are no words to describe my feelings of loss that day. I sank insensibly into my office chair, overcome with the strong despair that hardened upon me. The demons of reality fought for their rule, and for the first time in my life, I felt powerless.

I do not recall how long I sat in my office, nor who I called first. I only know that at some point in my sorrow, I strained enough composure to make flight arrangements for that evening. My brother John and I arrived in Miami at midnight, and left with my father and the dead body of my brother the following morning. I swore that day that I would find a way to honor Frankie in his death, as a man who offered so much in his life.

I found an appropriate tribute four years after Frankie's death. I purchased one hundred and forty acres of land in Huntington Valley, Pennsylvania. Only minutes from Frankie's former Upper Moreland home, I divided fifty acres between a shopping center and two hundred sixty-five stucco, tudor-style duplex homes, calling the development *Justa Farms*. Directly behind *Justa Farms* were ninety wooded acres, worth about one million dollars. It was donated as a parkland in the name of Frank J. Pileggi.

Once achieving park status, I developed the land in stages, eventually adding a snack bar and restrooms. Throughout the years, my progressive involvement offered the necessary finances for the lighted basketball

Justa Farms, Montgomery County, PA.
The ***Frank J. Pileggi Park***, *adjacent to **Justa Farms**, was named as a tribute to the author's much-loved brother.*

courts, soccer field, bleachers, digital scoreboard, picnic tables and playground equipment that exist today. The *Frank J. Pileggi Park* now rests proudly in the state registry for Montgomery County. I frequent the park alone in search of ball games, amazed at how anonymous children can trigger such familiar memories of my brother.

Looking back, I wonder if Frankie knew his time would be cut short. He realized the brevity of life and enjoyed it to the fullest, tempting others to do the same. At the age of thirty-nine, Frankie wrote the following, illustrating his beliefs and spirit:

> I do not choose to be a COMMON MAN; it is my right to be uncommon.
>
> If I can, I seek OPPORTUNITY, not security.
>
> I do not wish to be kept a citizen, HUMBLED and dulled by having the state look after me.
>
> I want to take a CALCULATED risk: to DREAM, to BUILD, to FAIL, and to SUCCEED.
>
> I refuse to barter INCENTIVE for a dollar.
>
> I prefer the CHALLENGE of life to the guaranteed existence: the thrill of FULFILLMENT to the stale calm of UTOPIA.
>
> I will not trade my FREEDOM nor my DIGNITY for a handout.
>
> I will never COWER before any master, nor bend to any threat.
>
> It is my heritage to stand erect, PROUD and unafraid, to think and act for MYSELF and to enjoy the benefit of my CREATIONS.

Today, my office continues to host Frankie's framed message, now yellowed with age, yet thriving with meaning. I conduct my life from his old desk given to me over thirty years ago when his newly remodeled office forbid him to keep it. I can place my hand on that desk and still feel the warmth of Frankie's hand from decades ago. An 8" x 10" photo of his teasing smile rests behind me. It is often mistaken to be of Tony Bennett and I confirm that Tony Bennett did, in fact, look like my brother.

Two weeks after Frankie's death, lack of appetite and lack of sleep was destroying me as it plucked away at the last of my fighting spirit. I withdrew from family and friends, attempting to focus solely on the distractions of business, but failing to find its previous comfort. Through Frankie's memory, I struggled with life's varied challenges and eventually accepted a distraction from business, a diversity of experience.

Frankie

Chapter 5

EDGAR AND JOAN (HOLLYWOOD)

Only weeks after Frankie's death, I got a call from Joan Rivers' manager and husband, Edgar Rosenberg. Edgar called in response to my forgotten scribbled note of interest left in Vegas. After a brief phone introduction, he began to inform me of *Rabbit Test* and its all-star cast, including Joan Rivers, Vincent Price, Paul Lynde, Jimmy Walker and Roddy McDowell. At my request, Edgar agreed to send a copy of the film's script.

Rabbit Test began with a typical storyline about a lonely boy who has his first sexual experience—a one-night stand on a pinball machine. Billy Crystal, in his feature film debut, played the lead as Lionel, whose world is turned upside down when he becomes the first pregnant man. I read the script in two hours, predicting it a comical success with a harmless PG-rating.

Edgar's follow-up telephone call secured my initial verbal commitment to a $150,000 investment. Before the conversation's end, Edgar extended a five-day invitation to California. I looked forward to the change of pace. After failing to convince Liz to leave the children, I left alone in March to meet Edgar face to face for the first time.

Edgar and I hit it off immediately. He held grandeur beyond his height, with a remarkable intelligence etched through his largely pronounced features. His cadaverous complexion reinforced full rounded lips, a delicate Jewish modeled nose, and eyes large and luminous beyond comparison. As a well-educated man, he expressed his depth of thought through articulate speech. His composed perfectionism in professional and personal affairs earned my respect within the first few days of our meeting. While I was visiting, one of his investors backed out at the last minute. I wrote a check for the additional $150,000, committing myself to one-third of the movie's total production cost on a handshake alone. Edgar offered a written contract, but I refused as an illustration of my faith in his integrity and character.

Edgar's British hospitality paralleled his class. He encouraged me to return to California in April for thirty days to spend on the Culver City Studio set of *Rabbit Test*, insisting on sharing his knowledge of movies in exchange for my knowledge of real estate. I accepted the offer, leaving my building business in the competent hands of my secretary, Helen, and my foreman. When I arrived in California, Edgar was waiting at the airport. We picked up as if we had been friends forever.

Edgar allowed me to keep my Hollywood promise to Frankie, despite his death. Frankie's 8" x 10" photo was used as a prop on the desk of the President of the United States, played by George Gobel. Edgar taught

me the production end of film, illustrating the impor-
tance of editing, lighting, camera angles, and direction.
While on the set, my experience in labor relations made
me chief negotiator in settling a walkout by members
of the Screen Extras Guild. I soon realized a basic simi-
larity between producing a Hollywood film with an
all-star cast and running my own building business—
both required the ability to deal with people in handling
heavy labor relations.

Rabbit Test was finally released in the fall of 1978,
earning me a ten percent profit. The film was later
considered by the media to be a bomb; however, my relationship with Edgar was a success. He introduced a
whole new world for me in film production. In return
for that education, I shared my expertise in real estate,
which resulted in a partnership for many future
projects. Eventually, Edgar invested in ninety-two of my
Justa Farms duplexes. They were sold only six years
ago, generating a tremendous profit for Joan.

Edgar was a loner. Beside his wife, Joan, and
daughter, Melissa, he had no family of his own. We
quickly adopted each other as brothers, corresponding
regularly by phone and rotating monthly trips to opposite coasts. Edgar filled the gap left by Frankie as we
continued with similar excursions for good food, worthy
charities, shared humor, and newly discovered ventures
in each other's career of building and film.

By the end of 1979, we intended on combining our
two careers through the construction of *Two Ponds*, a
one-hundred-million-dollar movie studio and condo
complex in Northampton Township of Bucks County,
Pennsylvania. It was to reside on eighty-seven acres of
cornfields, which I had purchased at the age of twenty-
one. The development called for fifteen buildings, with
thirty condos in each, ranging in price from $100,000
to $1 million per condo. In addition to a thirty-thousand-

square-foot sound stage and studio, there was to be a nine-hole golf course, tennis courts, and fulltime security, along with boating and fishing in the two man-made ponds already present.

The key to *Two Ponds* was not only to attract movie people through the available studio space, but also to offer the amenities suitable to the high rolling Hollywood types. Since my experience with *Rabbit Test*, my interest in film production, and even more so, my interest to produce a film on the east coast, had increased. I found the price of Hollywood extreme for its results and figured Bucks County had not yet been explored for its own film potential. I knew that the success of a Bucks County film would gain supporters for the *Two Ponds* studio and decided to pursue the new challenge.

Following weeks of unsuccessful brainstorming, an Abscam newspaper article, read on a return flight from California, triggered my movie's conception. I asked the flight attendant for a pen and paper and began to write *Uncle Scam*, a send up on Abscam and comical satire on the general corruption of politicians. Although the film is dated in the early eighties, my experiences over the years have proved its subject matter to be timeless.

I completed the script and continued as sole financier, hiring a limited local crew, including industrial filmmaker, Michael Levanios Jr., to assist me as co-director. The film cast consisted of twenty-seven Philadelphia area actors, featuring John Russel and Tommy McCarthy as FBI agents, and Maxine Green as McCarthy's wife. Russel received continued recognition in the 80's with *Honkytonk Man* and *Pale Rider*, while McCarthy has credited himself just recently as Bob Banks in the 2000 film *Meet the Parents*.

The only outside actors used in *Uncle Scam* were Joan Rivers, making a cameo appearance, and comedian

Pat Cooper, who played the head of the Justice Department. I used Cooper's role to again include Frankie in a film. Placed on his character's desk, Cooper addressed the same 8"x10" photo of Frankie used in *Rabbit Test*.

Using four neighborly locations, including my own home, the film was shot in only twenty-one days. However, the editing and final touches procrastinated its release by a year. The final result was a film produced entirely in Bucks County for only $250,000, one-fourth of the cost of Edgar's Hollywood production. After deciding to distribute the film myself, it opened in North Philadelphia's New Orleans theatre in 1981, the same time that pressure was increasing for *Two Ponds*.

Although reaching eighteen states, the film never generated rave reviews or a huge profit. *Uncle Scam* was an experiment to prove that a feature film could be conceived and produced from start to finish in the Bucks County area. In that sense, the film was a great success, drawing increased support for the development of the *Two Ponds* studio.

For three years, Edgar, Joan, and I continued to argue for the project in terms of the employment and income it would bring to the Philadelphia area. Township residents and officials continued to argue against the project in terms of its impact on their small, rural municipality. Despite a commitment from MGM to film five to ten pictures a year, extensive media coverage, and backing from the arts, by 1982, Edgar and I had realized that we were ahead of our time. The township had denied our final request to the zoning changes necessary for the project with the bottom line falling on traffic and other infrastructure-related problems.

After such a fully fought battle, we gracefully accepted our defeat. Shortly after, I began to slowly develop *Two Ponds* into million-dollar custom homes, bringing the tradition of the Southern estate to the pastoral lands of Bucks County. Completed in eight years, it is one of my proudest developments, located on the exclusive Beverly Hills Drive. A gated entrance takes you onto a private road with a lighted covered bridge, leading to the eight estates, each on ten or more acres. Each home is equipped with the grace of a carved staircase, a dramatic second floor balcony, library, solarium, three fireplaces, and other luxurious amenities. Edgar had intended on buying the most elaborate of the homes, until Joan's recurring appearances on *The Tonight Show* with Johnny Carson skyrocketed their careers.

Since his marriage to Joan in 1965, Edgar dedicated himself to guiding her career, refining her act for increasingly larger audiences. By 1983, Joan was a top Vegas headliner with sold-out concerts at Carnegie Hall,

The author, Edgar Rosenberg, and Joan Rivers
*on the set of **Rabbit Test**.*

several comedy albums, and two bestselling books. After eighteen years since her first appearance on *The Tonight Show* and several bouts as substitute host, NBC broke tradition, giving Joan a contract as permanent and sole co-host for Carson.

Joan's rising career and my friendship with Edgar took me deeper into the heart of Hollywood, rubbing elbows with the likes of Frank Sinatra, George Burns, Bob Hope, Jack Lemmon, and Dyan Canon. I enjoyed my fling with Hollywood, but began to witness Edgar's health deteriorate with the increased pressure of Joan's career, and intensified by his own need for perfection. Toward the end of 1984, Joan called to tell me of Edgar's revival after initially being pronounced dead from a massive heart attack.

Unable to handle the loss of another brother, I flew to meet Edgar at his bedside. I stayed the week, assuring myself of his stabilized condition before feeling comfortable enough to return to Pennsylvania. Within the month, Edgar called, expressing an unexplainable urgency to see me. His mysterious request was voiced through an unfamiliar tone, sounding contemplative and lacking his normal certainty. The lingering fear for Edgar's life took me back on a plane to California.

I arrived to find Edgar alone in his Bel Aire home. He greeted me with vivacious warmth full of unspoken words, before directing me to a full snifter of poured Bourbon. Despite my general dislike for alcohol, I accepted the gesture, taking a seat on the sofa where I had suspected he had previously been lying. After exchanging the normal courtesies between lapses of anticipating silence, Edgar began to divulge his extraordinary tale of an out-of-body experience.

Edgar had known of his momentary death before the doctors informed him that he flatlined. His one-minute-twelve-second lapse in life was timeless in the world he witnessed. Edgar's previous agnosticism was converted in a weightless wonder of luminous lights and majestic music. He remembered seeing my brother Frankie and his own parents, along with the feeling of absolute peace. It was a peace rarely felt within Edgar's own life on earth. He was a man who never made allusion to his previous life abroad. But, I knew that he was a German born Jew forced in flight to South Africa as a child during World War II. I always believed that you should not question things to which there are no answers. I never questioned Edgar's experience. I merely listened and offered company to his seclusion.

Edgar's experience gave him a new found fearlessness in life, especially when discussing his pending death. He also began to expose an emotional fragility previously hidden under his perfectionist nature. Edgar became more sensitive to the people and experiences surrounding him. However, one thing remained unchanged, his endless drive for Joan's success. A year after his heart attack, his incessant work for Joan's spotlight paid off.

Joan began to transform her comical style from self-deprecation to the lampooning of public figures, focusing on weight and fashion. She herself became an advocate for high fashion and plastic surgery. With the change in image, Joan and Edgar found increasing opportunities. By 1985, the new Fox Broadcasting Network offered Joan her own talk show, along with a three-year, fifteen-million-dollar contract. Edgar was named producer of *The Late Show Starring Joan Rivers*, a direct competitor with Johnny Carson's *The Tonight Show*.

Emotions ran high from the start, when Carson publicly rejected Joan and her career move. The press played Joan as a betrayer of Carson, her supposed benefactor, contributing to the public image of Joan as a sneak—sneaking away unannounced from NBC and Carson.

I flew out to catch the show's opening in October of 1986 and witnessed troubles immediately. Joan and Edgar continuously fought with Fox head, Barry Diller. Their three egos clashed continuously in a triangular ring of shouting matches. The behavior behind the scenes led me to predict an unavoidable tragedy. For the duration of my stay, I failed to voice my objections, remaining only supportive of their new show and their new success. But, when returning home to Pennsylvania, I sat at my desk and wrote the following thought-out letter of advice to Joan and Edgar:

Dear Joan & Edgar,

I felt I had to write to both of you and hope you understand the points I am trying to put across to you. Life is too short to be bickering and fighting with people. Wars are won and wars are lost, but the bottom line in the end is Japan and the United States are friends today. What a waste of life on both sides. It doesn't make sense, why? People misunderstand each other. No two people are the same. People are their own worst enemies. When you have a problem, which you have had many of them, Fox, etc., etc., etc. The other side is not as bad as you lead your minds to believe. People have a way of mentally making things worse than they really are. If you would take a guy like Diller and be nice to him, as much as you do not like him for things that he has said and done, and think about the things you have said and done and sit down and have dinner with him, possibly invite him to your home for dinner, you may find out he is not as bad as you lead yourselves to believe.

People can be rotten to each other and end up saying things to each other that lead to hatred, why? The lack of proper communication, egos, power happy, making points with their superiors or to each other, shameful. There are a lot of people we dislike, but we shouldn't get heart attacks over it, silly.

You are in business to make a living and enjoy the fruits of your creations. Don't ruin it for yourselves. Be happy you have achieved what you have so far. It is better, in some cases, to swallow rather than to spit something out. The other side could slip on the spit and get hurt and come back and spit on you.

As much as it hurts, you must be diplomatic and never ever let the other side know how you really feel. The other side may end up being your closest friend. Unfortunately, the whole world is run by the mouth, but should be run by the brain. Think before saying something you will be sorry for later.

Love & Kisses,
Tom

———◆———

Neither Joan nor Edgar thought twice of my suggestions. The spontaneity of the show's live format and Joan's unique brand of humor sustained the eight-month run of The Late Show with Joan Rivers. However, moderate ratings and increasing arguments with Diller led to their final dismissal from Fox in July of 1987. Security escorted Edgar off the lot, while Joan remained behind in an unsuccessful attempt at a solo reconciliation with Diller. Joan was replaced by Arsenio Hall and her name was dropped from the show's title. Edgar and Joan were devastated, and continued to blame each other.

The weight that the two placed on their careers was illustrated through premature threats of abandonment, both personal and professional. All of their arguments were ending with the threat of divorce and new management. I never realized how far everything got out of hand until Edgar's visit to Pennsylvania at the beginning of August.

Edgar arrived in an obviously frenzied emotional state accompanied with erratic behavior. His normal articulation in speech was interrupted by a series of non-sequential thoughts, causing him to stutter as he searched for the most common of words. Rather than taking trips of leisure, he took me with him to review old business records, making sure to tie up any loose ends. I assumed that he was taking precautions in case of a divorce, until I found him looking over his insurance policies for suicide coverage. When questioned, he was honest about his intentions. For three days, I was careful not to leave his side. When he retired to his Four Seasons Hotel room in Philadelphia those nights, I made no secret of the security hired to monitor his room.

I also made no secret of telling Edgar that I called his psychiatrist in California. He had been seeing this psychiatrist since his death experience to get his emotions and thoughts in hand. The doctor seemed to know something I did not and dismissed my concerns, assuring me that Edgar would never commit suicide. I was not satisfied with this, so I called Joan. Joan was more receptive to my alarm, yet, like his doctor, insisted that Edgar would never commit suicide. She remained confident that their arguments were part of any normal marriage and would be reconciled. I do not believe that Edgar ever viewed them the same. Edgar saw the arguments as more terminal, as preliminary stages to an unavoidable separation.

By the fourth day of Edgar's visit, he began to appear more at ease. He was returning to the confident and articulate friend I had known. I imagined that he had been comforted in my reported conversation with Joan, when he agreed that he would never be able to commit suicide. I was still not completely assured, so I continued to keep my guard up. I discussed the option of bringing him to Jeanes Psychiatric Hospital in Philadelphia for professional care. It was an option, of course, that he denied.

I took him to his favorite Italian restaurant that evening and began to address his suicide threat from a new angle, a more personal and selfish angle. I still remember my exact words to Edgar: "You are my brother and I love you. If you won't live for yourself, than please do it for me." I added that I could not handle the loss of another brother, that I no longer had it in me. Edgar promised me that he would never hurt me like that and promised me that he would not commit suicide.

After dinner, I dropped him off at the hotel. We agreed that I would pick him up the following morning to take him to the airport. When he arrived home, he was to first talk to Joan and then seek professional help. He got out of the car, promising again that he would not do anything stupid. Half jokingly, I warned that if he did I would not attend his funeral. Much more assured of his well being, I drove down to my shore house in Ocean City, New Jersey, to be with my wife and children. I left for Ocean City feeling confident that Edgar would not lie to me and confident that he would be alive when I arrived in the morning.

I called Edgar at ten that evening, after I arrived at the shore. My family was already asleep and I was searching for assurance that would allow for my own sleep. I got it when Edgar answered the phone. He laughed at my persistence, insisting he was going to bed and would see me in the morning. I fell asleep on the living room sofa in front of our open sliding glass doors that overlooked the restful ocean and the starlit shore sky.

Shortly after midnight, I woke suddenly with an eerie feeling, like I was not alone. Instead of searching the house, something drew me past the already open glass doors to the balcony outside. The moon was near full, silvering the white sand below. My eyes danced briefly with the lights from the summer sky, until distracted by a celestial discrepancy. It had all the familiarity of a star, but it was brighter and appeared much closer. Focusing on its brilliance, I watched as it shot up into the vibrant night sky. It appeared to be a shooting star headed in the wrong direction and fading with its distance. I continued to witness the starry merriment through tired eyes, dismissing the incident as an unanswerable phenomenon, before retiring again to bed.

At six o'clock in the morning, I called Edgar with my keys in hand to let him know that I was on my way. I received no answer. In light of the week's conversations, I wasted no time in calling security, with the hopes that he was probably at breakfast. They put me on hold for twenty minutes, while they searched for Edgar. A shuddering and indefinite fear crept into my blood. The security officer returned to the phone, telling me to get down there immediately. My mind raced faster than my Ford as I dodged through the surrealism of slow motion traffic. I arrived at the Four Seasons one hour later, cutting my normal drive time in half. The police were already there. After I offered identification, they allowed me to enter Edgar's hotel room. I stared before me at vacancy, for nothing was to be seen, but Edgar in his blue pajamas curled across the floor.

Edgar killed himself in old-fashioned Hollywood style, mixing alcohol with an overdose of his prescription Valium. Before his death, he recorded three tapes, one for his daughter, one for Joan, and one for me. I stayed long enough for the officers to play my tape and heard Edgar blame his suicide on an excess of ambition and pride that had become contradictory to his circumstance. From the tape, I learned that Edgar was in the process of recording when I called him the previous night.

Mid-tape, Edgar's hollow voice was interrupted with the phone's ring and a brief pause in taping. He resumed his recording after our conversation, saying:

> "Dear Tom, the phone you just heard ringing was your call. You are the sweetest man on earth and I feel terribly, terribly guilty of imposing upon you, but I think of you as my only brother. The only brother I have ever had, the only man that I can really trust who understands me and who thinks like me, and who I would put my hand in the fire for, and I know you would do the same."

———◆———

Edgar was my brother and the imposition to which he referred was Joan. Edgar left me the responsibility to protect Joan from the "barracudas" and "stupid money mistakes," after he placed the principal of his insurance money in Melissa's name.

With the tapes, Edgar left a one-page letter, stating his name, address, phone number, and my name as the first person to contact. It was dated August 13, 1987 at midnight. I often wonder if my rising star the night before had been Edgar, finally finding his peace within the universe.

Immediately after the suicide, I experienced great unrest from media bombardment at my home and office.

To escape the disturbances, I disappeared for a week on a friend's houseboat in Atlantic City. I spent that entire week alone, with only the recorded voice of Edgar. I listened to the tape over and over again, trying to find meaning behind his words and understanding behind his actions. The tape is transcribed below, in its entirety, so that the reader might also find meaning and understanding.

————◆————

Dear Tom,

I hope you don't think worse of me for doing what I have done, but I just couldn't see myself living under the circumstances which were facing me. You and I have talked this out many a time, and I think if you were in my shoes you would be doing the same thing. I cannot bear to live as a fifth wheel—I have too much ambition, I have too much pride. Pride can kill somebody, but it's all I have.

I am proud of what I have done, I am proud of what I have accomplished, and I cannot see myself shunted aside and thrown on the garbage heap because of age or because of my illness. I know that this is done unintentionally by Joan, who is going through her own emotional crisis, her mid-life crisis, she's gone through terrible shock. So don't blame her, she's gone through tremendous traumatic experiences of being fired off the show. She thinks her career is over, which I don't believe it is. She will always be in the forefront of comedy. She is the only woman around who is doing it, who can do it, and she will pop up again. Because of my death, she will have a hard couple of months, maybe even a year, where it will be very difficult for her to go on stage and make jokes.

So, please help her financially in a sense that even though I said give all the four million to Melissa upon my death—the four million life insurance—make sure that Joan either gets a loan or gets part of it—I'll leave it to you. But don't force her to give up the house, and go back to work where perhaps the best thing for her career would be if she would just disappear for a year, but in order to do that she needs financial help. So either sell some of the houses, or use some of the four million, or give her the interest of the four million, but keep the principal in Melissa's name, but I'll leave that to you to work out with Joan and Melissa. But don't be harsh on Joan. Please, please, please look after my Melissa.

---◆---

Dear Tom,

The phone that you just heard ring was your call. You are the sweetest man on earth and I feel terribly, terribly guilty of imposing upon you, but I think of you as my only brother. The only brother I have ever had, the only man that I can really trust who understands me and who thinks like me, and who I would put my hand in the fire for, and I know you would do the same. And I hope that you would understand that I would always do that.

What I am about to do is going to upset you. Please don't think too badly of me, but as I said before I cannot live as a fifth wheel. I love Joan too much, I cannot see myself shunted aside. I know I am hurting Melissa, but if I don't do it now, I am just postponing the inevitable. I am not going to see myself institutionalized and even after three or four weeks in the hospital, it's not going to be the same again because Joan is what she is and she's going through her problems and I am not the one to help her. So do me a big favor, protect her from the gay guys, protect her from the fags. They will try and slice her up, they will try and grab things from her. For my sake, protect her, invest the money wisely,

Husband it for her and for Melissa, and protect her from herself and protect her from the barracudas that are going to come swimming around, the lawyers, the accountants, and everybody else. You know the group. You have been through it. You've seen them. Protect her from the agents and don't let her make stupid money mistakes. See that she doesn't want financially, that she doesn't have to give up the house immediately—but also as I say, protect Melissa's little nest egg.

I love you and I have a feeling I'll be seeing you soon. But you ought to stay alive to make sure that everybody is on track and everything is taken care of, but eventually I know that in the next life you and I will link arms again and be kissing each other again. I love you very, very, very much and goodbye, goodbye, goodbye.

Tom, one other thing while I think of it. Please get after Bobby Griffbaum to sit on that cancellation of that three million dollars and get Joan to write him a letter reinstating the three million dollars because if anything happens to Joan, Melissa should have that extra protection.

Again, my eternal love, my love to your children. I don't know what else to say to you other than I will always love you and treasure you and keep you in my memories. Please think kindly of me and think of me once in a while. Bye bye.

I returned home after my week alone, having forgiven Edgar for his broken promise of life. As a man of my word, I kept my promises to him. I did not attend his funeral and I offered guidance and money to both Joan and her career.

Edgar had asked me to help Joan financially in the event that she may need a year away from the spotlight to recover the emotional trauma. Against my advice, Joan returned to her career two weeks after Edgar's death in search of financial independence. As one who buries my own sorrow in the distractions of business, I was one of the few to respect Joan's decision, despite my disapproval. The move became a public relations nightmare with Joan portrayed by the media as an image-crazed woman with little sentiment for her dead husband. Opportunity disappeared with public sympathy and Joan re-situated herself in New York, trying her hand in Broadway.

After a year of Joan's Broadway success in Neil Simon's *Broadway Bound*, I began discussions in her behalf with Tribune Entertainment. By 1989, Tribune launched Joan in her own syndicated daytime talk show, distinct in its emphasis on gossip. She illustrated her appreciation of my efforts by keeping my picture visible on *The Joan Rivers Show* set. In response to audience curiosity over the unnamed photo, I appeared as a guest on the show, described as the man "who had saved her life." Perhaps it was Joan who had saved mine. The huge responsibility of her career had kept Edgar's memory alive, supplying me time to resolve my own feelings of guilt. I still dream about Edgar often and haunt myself with the unanswerable, "What if?"

Chapter 6

A DEN OF THIEVES

oan's show came at an opportune time. It temporarily relieved me from her career concerns for growing business concerns of my own. In 1989, I was a director of the Cheltenham Bank board for nine years, after being drafted in 1980 by the President and Chairman of the Board, Monroe Long. Monroe was a man older in years, who I had known since my first Cheltenham savings account at the age of six.

When I turned sixteen, he was the one to approve the unforgettable loan that launched my building career. Throughout the years, we established an ongoing business relationship. After he brought me onto the Cheltenham Board, it became a friendship, when Monroe took the role of mentor and showed me the ropes to banking.

I was brought onto the board at the age of thirty-five. I was the youngest and least formally educated of the board members. I felt that I had to prove myself, working twice as hard for the bank's success and quickly earning the hesitant respect of my colleagues, most more than twenty years my senior. I enjoyed my years on Cheltenham's board, priding myself in the association with a one-hundred-year-old Montgomery County community bank. The security of my building business allowed Cheltenham to dominate my time, obligating myself to the loan, salary, and building committees, while refusing to ever accept a director's fee. My service was not for money, but for the advancement of the bank and its employees, many of which I had known since my youth.

When the bank looked to move from Central Avenue to Huntington Pike, I offered to build their new headquarters for half of a million dollars below the lowest bid. I built it for cost, calling in favors and taking no profit for myself. I used my connections to drum up business for the bank through reliable loans and hefty accounts. The bank employees would joke, "Tom Pileggi is Cheltenham Bank." The truth was that Cheltenham Bank was a community bank, belonging to the people, or so I thought. I was merely one of those people and viewed Cheltenham as part of my roots.

In 1985, I was honored with Cheltenham Bank's highest award of a gold clock, which read, "In grateful appreciation of Tom Pileggi's tireless, capable and unselfish efforts in the building and expansion of this bank." One year after being presented the award, I was drafted to the board of Cheltenham's parent company, Independence Bancorp, Inc.

I had been opposed to INBC's acquisition of Cheltenham Bank four years earlier and voiced my opinion openly. Cheltenham Bank had its own success and established reputation in meeting community needs. Bank executives and officers were won over with the promise of a larger purse, so by 1982, we had joined five other banks as a subsidiary of INBC. When I was offered the opportunity to serve on the parent board in 1986, I saw it as an opportunity to protect the interest of Cheltenham.

I openly objected to wasted money, bad loans, and shady characters during my three years on the INCB board, which left many ruffled feathers. I continued to represent and defend Cheltenham Bank among the representatives of Bucks County Bank, Third Bank of Scranton, Lehigh Valley Bank, and the soon to pull out, Freedom Valley Bank. Bucks County, the largest bank, with an ego to match, held control over the rest. They labeled Cheltenham the "down-towners," despite our consistent financial success and Bucks' consistent bad loans.

The bottom line was that INBC was losing money as a whole. All five banks had invested their money together through David Astheimer, the sole investor for the entire corporation. For three years, I would observe David when he met with the INBC Board to review the status of our funds. David was a young, Harvard graduate and I did not trust him from the start. He never looked anyone in the eye and used technical and complex terms as a matter of fact, leaving the elderly board too embarrassed of their ignorance to question his authority. I once expressed my distrust of David to Monroe, but he dismissed it as my own paranoia. When the board approached me in the summer of 1990 to serve on INBC's Funds Management and Auditing Committees, I jumped at the chance.

My first day on the Funds Management Committee was scheduled to begin at a 9:00 a.m. meeting in the INBC headquarters. I arrived two hours early to prepare, reviewing the investment portfolios made available to all board members. INBC was a three-billion-dollar organization with a two-hundred-million dollar net worth. I reviewed the paperwork, figuring the numbers and calculations in my head. My math led me to the conclusion that INBC was eighty-five million dollars under water. If the corporation was sold that day, we would have lost almost half of our net worth as a result of junk bonds, failed securities, and overall poor investments that lay solely in the hands of David Astheimer. More importantly, the eighty-five million dollar loss went unreported.

Carl Biddleman, the chair of the committee, was the first to arrive at the meeting. As a professor of finance at Lehigh University, he was well respected for his expertise. I reported my findings to a very straight-faced Carl. He told me not to worry and that we would eventually get the money back. Surprised at his nonchalance, I repeated the total of the loss, seeking some sort of confirmation. Carl said that technically I was right; there was a loss, but nothing to be concerned over. He then dismissed me as "ridiculous" to find such problems on my *first day* on the committee.

I dismissed Carl Biddleman's confidence of retrieval and revealed my findings to all twenty-three members of the INBC Board at a later one o'clock meeting. On the basis that David Astheimer was the only individual responsible for two hundred million dollars of the corporation's assets, I demanded that an investigative committee be assigned. I received disapproval from every member of the board that day for going against the well-respected Carl. However, I did win the approval of an investigative committee by two votes.

The committee consisted of one board member representing each bank. The board agreed that my "big mouth" earned my place on the committee as a Cheltenham representative. We began a detailed investigation, analyzing investments and portfolios while interviewing co-workers, business associates, and brokerage firms in relation with David. We found that David had been taking kick backs from different brokerage firms buying securities. At the completion of each business day, winners were placed into his personal account, while the losers were placed into INBC's account. David was originally stubborn in his admission of guilt, until the evidence against him became undisputable.

By November 1990, the entire board was convinced of David's fraud and the resulting financial loss. A meeting was called to discuss necessary action. At the onset of the meeting, INBC's representative and director took the floor in a drawn-out passionate speech, encouraging a cover-up as the only means to maintain our board seats, as well as their director's fees. Essentially, he was asking us all to break the law, by keeping the eighty-five-million-dollar loss hidden from the public and stockholders.

I addressed him and the rest of the board, informing them that the proposed plan was illegal. It was our fiduciary responsibility as board directors to publicly report the loss. There was silence in the boardroom as each member acquired collaboration from one another through meaningful glances. Their body language seemed to indicate support for him, so before they were given the opportunity to verbalize it, I told them that I would not do it and left the meeting with my blood pressure soaring.

Monroe Long, who by that time, was Chairman of INBC, as well as for Cheltenham, raced after me to the street, stopping me in my tracks and telling me to calm down. I told Monroe that I would not take any part in a cover-up. Without any attempt to persuade me differently, he told me to do what I had to, but that he would deny ever saying it. I was not actually sure of what I had to do, so I returned to my Warrington office and called an old friend.

Dick Ritter was an FBI agent. Our relationship had begun fifteen years before, when the FBI came to me for information on a union problem in Bucks County. I continued to offer my cooperation and assistance throughout the years to both the FBI and Dick. When Dick retired, our relationship continued more personally through casual lunches. I was counting on his advice when I left the board meeting that day and called Dick at home, later that day.

I related everything that was going on at INBC— the investigation of David, the multimillion dollar loss, and the talk of a cover-up. Dick assured me that I was doing the right thing by reporting it. The next day, the FBI went in and hit INBC hard, examining all their files and conducting their own investigation on David. David Astheimer was convicted of conspiracy to fraud and served three years in prison. Basically, he had robbed the bank of eighty-five million dollars, using only his phone and pen.

I was up for re-election on both boards in December of 1990. After the previous month's events, I did not anticipate being voted back on either board, nor did I care. I was totally disillusioned with the entire organization and began to disassociate myself from both Cheltenham and INBC.

On December 19, I delivered my written resignation to Monroe. Monroe informed me that I had been voted back on both boards and asked me to reconsider. Cheltenham Bank had to start consolidating by cutting expenses and salaries. My personal rapport with the employees would ease some upcoming blows. I declined Monroe's offer, feeling it was time for the board to earn their fees and take responsibility for their own actions. I had served a loyal ten years for Cheltenham bank and was now ready to return to my own business and my family.

Chapter 7

THE BATTLE BEGINS

The year after my resignation, I continued with Joan's career, developed a refreshed focus on building, and spent much overdue time with my family. I put my experience with INBC behind me and enjoyed the freedom that came with it.

Toward the end of 1992, I was surprised to receive a call from Monroe, asking me to return to the Cheltenham and INBC Boards. INBC's capital and earnings were rapidly decreasing due to the diseased Bucks County and Lehigh Valley Banks. INBC was consistently pulling the capital from Cheltenham to support the bad investments and bad loans made by Bucks County Bank. Although independently successful, Cheltenham and Scranton were being taken down the drain with INBC as a whole.

As a solution to their financial troubles, INBC was considering the consolidation of Bucks County Bank with Cheltenham Bank. I cared little for Bucks or INBC, but was still haunted with a devotion to Cheltenham and its employees. I had witnessed the lifelong dedication of employees like Josephine Cotignola, Mildred Sweeney, Dennis Clarke, Paul Brenner, and Hank Ashworth. There was also Jack Young, Gordon Long, Doug Adams, Danny Gabbamonte, Ed McDual, and forgive me for not mentioning the so many other dedicated employees that would consume the bulk of my pages. The consolidation of banks would mean an inevitable loss of these jobs, along with the loss of the Cheltenham name.

In December 1992, despite my family's infinite objections, I agreed to return to the Cheltenham board only. As an officer of both Cheltenham and INBC, Monroe's conflict of interest left him exempt from any attempt at sparing Cheltenham's name. I returned as a director with the sole intention of saving the bank from oblivion. Within the Cheltenham Board, we established the informal "Cheltenham Group." This wholly independent group was comprised of board members interested in acquiring Cheltenham's independence from INBC. We did not meet as a board, but as an ad hoc committee concerned for the future of Cheltenham Bank. The group consisted of long time board members Harry Barbin, Ron Froggatt, Ken Greenwood, Bob Hunter, Carl Hahn, Hugh Taylor, Mickey Schrenk, and myself, Thomas Pileggi. While Hunter, Barbin, Long, and Schrenk also continued to hold seats on the INBC Board, I took the lead in preparing for our behind the scenes battle.

With intentions of saving the bank, Monroe pushed for approval and extended me, in the name of Cheltenham, a six-and-a-half-million-dollar credit, as ammunition to go to war. I obtained another seven million through other banks and associations, all of which went toward the gradual acquisition of stock. I began to spend my own time and money on an analysis of

Cheltenham's financial worth, valuing it at forty-seven to fifty million dollars. Since Cheltenham was a subsidiary of INBC, I began to buy INBC stock. My plan was to acquire enough stock that INBC would see us as a proposed threat and eventually agree to sell Cheltenham independently.

Harry Barbin was not only a board member, but also the legal representative for Cheltenham. As our lawyer, Barbin began to set up meetings between our group, with me as spokesman, and INBC that would continue from January 1993 until November of the same year. In May 1993, INBC hired the Manhattan Consulting Co. to determine a means of more profitability. The result was the *Manhattan Report* with its general thrust being the consolidation of all banks into one principal bank. The heat intensified as our meetings proved unproductive.

At a Cheltenham Group meeting in June 1993, Harry Barbin suggested we bring in Fred Dreher, an outside attorney from Duane, Morris & Hechscher in Philadelphia. Dreher was an old law partner of Barbin's and was hired to explore our legal options in transacting the repurchase of Cheltenham from INBC. Our meeting with Dreher confirmed that Cheltenham could only be bought with the increased acquisition of stock. Dreher also suggested contracting Hopper Soliday, an investment-banking firm, for an analysis on the worth of INBC and Cheltenham, as well as for a plan to purchase evaluation. I offered my financial support for the analysis, interested in the discrepancies between their findings and my own. By July, the Cheltenham Group was in full accordance on the purchase of Cheltenham and I had purchased enough stock to approach INBC with a serious offer.

On July 5, 1993, I had Harry Barbin draw up a tender offer to Independence Bancorp's Chief Executive

Officer and President, John Harding. It stated our intent to either a) buy the holding copy, or b) buy Cheltenham independently from INBC. The theory was that my increased share of stock would put a fear in Harding. If they did not release Cheltenham, our only alternative would be to take the entire company. I had no desire to purchase the diseased INBC, but was willing to do so if necessary.

I only needed twelve percent of the stock to put me in the position to buy INBC. After receiving no response from my offer, I bought an additional forty thousand shares of INBC stock for $1,200,000 on July 6. I was well on my way and Harding began to sweat. A week later, Harding came back with an offer, although not the one we had anticipated. Harding said that he knew we did not want INBC, nor did he intend to sell. However, Cheltenham was another story. He gave us every impression that Cheltenham was for sale, telling me that if I called off the dogs by selling my stock, we could begin discussions. After gaining approval from the Cheltenham Group, I sold all but two hundred shares of stock by mid-August, believing it the only way to gain compliance from Harding.

Harding scheduled a meeting for the end of the month that he repeatedly postponed throughout September. I received a registered letter from him dated September 27, retracting any commitment to meet and turning down all offers to sell Cheltenham or INBC. Harding left me strapped. It was my understanding that as a director on Cheltenham, the entire month of October was a quiet period for buying stock. A quiet period is when any important event is going to occur in a corporation with public stockholders. As a board member of that corporation, we are advised not to trade in stock because we could be influenced by that event. This particular event was INBC's quarterly release of earnings and dividend action. We were not allowed to buy or sell stock until the information was made public. In other words, my hands were tied until November.

After receiving Harding's letter, I confronted Monroe Long as an officer of the INBC Board. Monroe told me that he was not the only one to deny my offer. The entire board had unanimously rejected the sale of Cheltenham. Essentially, he was saying that Hunter, Barbin, and Schrenk had all voted against me. Half of the Cheltenham Group were traitors. I had never made a move without first receiving full support from the Group, and now they turned their backs on me. We all started fighting in the same foxhole, but when the smoke cleared, I was alone.

I continued alone. I intended to pick up where I left off in November, again pursuing the purchase of INBC through twelve percent of stock. I disassociated myself from both the Cheltenham Board and the Cheltenham Group throughout October and the beginning of November, refusing to attend any of their meetings. Particularly, I refused to attend a Group meeting on November 1, 1993. The meeting was to be with Fred Dreher and his associate, Mary Mullany, and the proposed agenda was to discuss the feasibility, at that point, in obtaining Cheltenham by reviewing what was accomplished thus far. In my opinion, nothing had been accomplished. I refused the meeting and any of their calls, determined to do things my own way. I called Monroe that morning, telling him that I was waging my own war in buying stock.

On November 3, I began to reacquire INBC stock to build a position, purchasing ten thousand shares at an average of $27 per share. I bought another five thousand shares the next day at a decreased $25.75. I was prepared to pay up to $38.50 per share—my estimated maximum worth of the stock. At the time, I had enough liquidation to continue with the purchase of INBC on my own, determined to save Cheltenham and the two hundred and fifty jobs that came with it. My plan was to buy slowly, every few weeks from November to February, keeping the stock prices down.

Harry Barbin left a message with my secretary about a scheduled Group meeting for November 11. This meeting, to be held at Mickey Schrenk's office, would be the first that Hopper Soliday's analysis and plan of purchase would be made available. I decided to go to the meeting, for no other reason than to get a copy of the report. Fred Dreher, Mary Mullany, representatives of Hopper Soliday, and the rest of the Cheltenham Group were present. I arrived to the meeting late, interrupting Hopper Soliday's slide presentation, already in process.

Hopper Soliday had reached their concluding evaluation through public reports published quarterly. Within their analysis of INBC and Cheltenham, they included analysis of six larger banks, all likely candidates to merge with INBC in the future. Of these banks, PNC, Corestates, Fidelity, and Meridian were discussed, with Meridian being the most likely candidate. Hopper Soliday suggested that if INBC were to be taken over, we might have a better likelihood of purchasing Cheltenham independently through the larger corporation.

For the past year, there had been random talk of Independence Bancorp merging. During this time, INBC Board members assured the rest of us that INBC would remain independent, as their name suggests. Hopper Soliday's whole discussion relied on too many unlikely actions in the future, rather than definite actions in the present. I was resolute on immediate proceedings and took my chances as an independent operator. I obtained my copy of the analysis and left before the meeting was over.

Hopper Soliday's evaluation of the worth of Cheltenham and INBC was comparable to my own, confirming that I had done my homework and encouraging me to continue as planned. I was working toward purchasing five percent of the stock. When reached, as required by law, I would report to the U.S. Securities and Exchange Commission my intent on taking over the organization. On November 17, I bought an additional twenty thousand shares of INBC stock at $29.81 per share.

The following morning, I attended a formal Cheltenham Board meeting as strongly suggested by Monroe. At that meeting, Harry Barbin informed the board of INBC's intent to merge with Corestates Financial Corp. Barbin's voice held no reflection of chance or possibility, when he told us of a scheduled meeting with Corestates representatives that afternoon. He sounded definite, as if their minds were made up, without offering the respect of a board vote. At that point, I do not think we had any say in the matter, but I voted against the merger anyway.

Before the day's end, INBC had issued a press release in response to ongoing rumors and a call from the National Association of Securities Dealers, Inc., stating that INBC was in discussions with a third party regarding a possible acquisition. I went to bed late that evening, but doubt if I even closed my eyes. I arose before the sun dawned and drove to the local 7-11 for the daily edition of the *Philadelphia Inquirer*. On the first page of the business section, I read what Barbin had told us the day before, only excluding the third party's name: Independence Bancorp was in merger talks with another corporation.

I felt blood gush into my hollow cheeks, and a whirlwind of emotions raged inside me. I struggled to pay the clerk with tremulous hands and retreated to my car. I fought the clouding faces of the Cheltenham employees as they trudged through my mind. Mildred

Sweeney was in her seventies and worked as the President's secretary for fifty years. Josephine Gotignola was a single mother and a loan officer at Cheltenham for many years. The majority of employees were between the ages of fifty and seventy, many of them dedicating more than half of their lives to Cheltenham.

Now, it seemed likely that their positions would be erased with the bank's name. I tried to save a people's bank, making the mistake of believing it belonged to the people. I felt as if I had failed those people, after comforting them along the way with tales of Cheltenham's independence. Naively, I believed that the good guys always won. My conviction was lost, as I read my defeat to greed on the first page of the business section.

I thought of who I could call or where I could go, grasping for any last bit of fight left in me. At 5:30 a.m., faint and overburdened with a sickness in my heart, I returned home to the comfort of my wife. Liz put her own relief of the closing battle aside, relying on her faith in God, and offering her soft voiced consolations with her lips close to my ear. I searched for my own faith, struggling to find strength that would allow me to continue as if not already beaten.

When the stock market opened that morning, I made a direct call to my broker, Michael Acampora. Michael was Senior Vice President specializing in bank stocks at the brokerage firm, Robert W. Baird. I had been introduced to him over a decade ago through Cheltenham, and I shared him as a broker with the majority of the board. Michael was aware of the press release and told me that I had a fortune to make in the pending merger. Money was not the issue; integrity and values were. I sold all but two hundred shares of my stock, which I needed to keep my place on the board. I sold my stock as a message to the employees, a message that I could not be bought with the rest.

I refused to make a profit off the sale of INBC and donated my minimal stock earnings to charity. The merger was agreed upon and publicly announced at 3:47 p.m. that afternoon. The following day, the media flocked to the story and I was forced to listen to Acampora's scrutiny. The merger agreement proposed a stock swap at $40.50, an additional six dollars per share higher than what I had sold my stock for. While the majority of directors and executives were choosing personal profit over the future of their employees, I had gone to see my lawyer, the night before, in search of a class action suit to stop the merger.

Although it was not my lawyer's specialty, I asked Jerry Balka to put an injunction on the merger. I told him to use any means and acquire any assistance, as long as he could stop the merger. With the close to twenty thousand dollars I paid him, Balka sought counsel from an outside Philadelphia firm, experienced in that field. Within the week, the initial steps of the injunction were in progress.

By November 24, word got out on the injunction and I received separate phone calls from Monroe Long and John Harding. They were calling specifically on the behalf of the Chairman and Chief Executive Officer of Corestates, Terry Larsen. Larsen had been told of my intentions and was sending a warning. If I continued with the injunction or took any other means to interfere with the merger, all of the Cheltenham employees would lose their jobs. I never paid much mind to threats, but this one was a major concern. With the success of the injunction in question, I stood to lose everything I was working for, all of the jobs that I had fought to hold.

I had never met Larsen, nor did I know anything about the man. However, I did know that he was high up in a very large corporation and would find little time for a mere director of a small community bank. However, I obviously got Larsen's attention with the proposed injunction. Now, I had to find a way to secure a meeting. The meeting would exhaust my options, offering one last opportunity to either save the bank or buy the Cheltenham name. I did some basic investigations into Larsen and his past, looking for a commonality that could find my way into his office. I found that commonality in the form of Bud Hansen.

Bud Hansen and I had been friends for years, beginning with our similarly shared professions as real estate developer and builder. It turned out Hansen and Larsen were old acquaintances through an association with the Archdiocese of Philadelphia and Archbishop Bevilocqua. I made a call to Bud, explaining my situation. In turn, he called Larsen, asking him to meet with me. Larsen agreed and the meeting was set for November 30, 1993 at 2:00 p.m.

I met Larsen and his associate, Jim Carnie, at Larsen's Corestates office in Philadelphia. I was taken back by Larsen's mediocre appearance. This man of great power, that held the future of so many in his hands, lacked any physical presence of authority. At five-feet-ten-inches tall, he was about a hundred pounds oversized, and dressed in a poorly-fitted shirt and wide-short trousers confined at the waist with a belt. His remaining polished hair was swept to the side, anxious to hide the reflections of overhead light. He demonstrated a smile that seemed as hard to preserve as the shine on his shoes.

I imagined that Larsen was offering the pretense of respect for Bud Hansen's sake. After an exchange of professional courtesies, Larsen gave me the floor, allowing me to state my claim. I began the meeting by expressing my sincere concern for Cheltenham and its employees. Larsen responded, "It makes me feel good, Tom, that you are so concerned for your bank and your people." His tone was as average as his appearance, dull and slacked. Nonetheless, I gave him the benefit of the doubt, believing that he may be an honorable man with a bit of dignity and a bit of heart.

I continued to recount my battle in acquiring Cheltenham, detailing my efforts with each stock purchase. I advised him against the diseased Bucks and Lehigh Valley banks, while encouraging Cheltenham's independence. After giving him my portfolio on Cheltenham, containing all the research on its worth, I offered to buy it independently for sixty million dollars, ten million over its estimated value. I realize, now, that my biggest mistake that day was building Cheltenham up too well.

Larsen concluded our meeting thirty minutes after its start, telling me that he would see what he could do and get back to me. He added that if I called off the injunction, he could assure me one thing, "Cheltenham will remain Cheltenham." It would become Corestates' Cheltenham Bank, with all of its branches remaining and very few, if any, people would lose their jobs. He gave me his word and his handshake. I believe in a handshake, but I did not fully trust Larsen.

I went to the bank that afternoon to discuss the matter with the bulk of employees. The general agreement was, that if Cheltenham will remain as a subsidiary of Corestates with job security, the merger should be allowed to continue. That same day, I called Jerry Balka to cancel the process of injunction. Two days later, Jim Carnie called me to say, due to a polling of interest, Cheltenham was not for sale.

I never began with the intention of owning a bank. I began with the intention of saving jobs and the Cheltenham name. Larsen gave me his word that neither was in jeopardy, so Carnie's call merely seemed like the final resolution. It seemed that the battle was over and we had won. A month later, Larsen continued to speak in defense of the employees, offering the same assurance to them that he had offered to me the day of our meeting.

As President and Chairman of the Board, Monroe Long was too eager to accept all of Larsen's contracts. I knew Long and valued him and his wife as close friends for many years. Although I did not believe that Monroe would intentionally hurt me, or any other bank employee, I was surprised by his behavior associated with the merger. I wondered why he had brought me back onto the Cheltenham Board in the first place. Monroe claimed that he needed me to save Cheltenham from the claws of Bucks County Bank and took sincere measures to assist me in the process. Yet, he voted against me in my attempt to buy Cheltenham's independence. By doing so, Monroe sold out half of the Cheltenham Group, the group that he sponsored financially, while at the same time, increasing my credit.

Then, only a month later, at the start of November, I told Monroe that I was resuming the purchase of INBC stock with an intention to buy the Corporation. At that time, he must have been in the process of negotiations with Corestates, since the actual merger took place only nineteen days later. Still, Monroe, my mentor and friend, made no attempt to discourage my decision or tell me that I was a tiger chasing my own tail. Even though Monroe was torn between professional and personal responsibilities, his hopscotching around led me to one conclusion. Monroe was one of them, one of the greedy executives, a pawn in the game that willingly allowed profit to replace honor.

Terry Larsen revealed a similar character, when the Corestates/INBC merger was finally consummated in July of 1994. Larsen's word was worth as much as his handshake. All former INBC banks became Corestates Banks, and within a year, the majority of the employees were relieved from their positions. I did the best I could to find jobs for the lost employees: some at other banks, some in doctor's offices, some in real estate, and some as 7-11 clerks. Hank Ashworth, whose father was president of the bank before Monroe, was a loan officer in his sixties. Now, he does carpentry work. Bank executives, like Monroe, swiveled in their high paying board seats and false sense of security, as hearts and homes around them were broken.

Greed is a funny thing. I have always believed that what comes around goes around. Unfortunately, in Monroe's case, his time came too late. He already took every one down with him. Shortly after the merger consummation, Monroe was essentially told to get his car washed and cleaned. He was given his severance package and dismissed from the company. It was only then, when Monroe's own future was in question, that he said, "We should have listened to Tommy." At one time or another, we have all been caught in traps. We have all made decisions that we soon regret. It was a sad day for Monroe when he reflected on the person that a situation had forced him to become.

Larsen continued to publicly display his gluttonous character, selling Corestates to First Union three years later. When Larsen sold out Corestates, he sold out Philadelphia. He took a brief position as deputy chairman at First Union just before his early retirement, making a rumored fifty million dollars with stock options, plus one million dollars a year for life. It was my understanding that he took the money and retired to Hawaii.

I have drawn my own conclusions on Larsen. He made his millions as a traitor, not as a banker. He was in the right place at the right time, selling out enough people to make enough money for his fancy jackets and gold chains. I do not believe that Larsen could have ever have built a bank on his own. Banks rely on people; Larsen relied on money and power. My only wish for Larsen today is that his future reflects all of the decisions in his past.

When Corestates dropped the Cheltenham name, I bought it, starting the First Cheltenham Financial Corporation. I run First Cheltenham as a commercial mortgage lender, until the day I can branch off as a bank. Meanwhile, I take what business I can, catering to former Cheltenham clients and steering excess business to surrounding community banks and mortgage companies. My bank will progress the old fashioned way, starting from scratch. It will never become a Corestates or a First Union, nor do I care it to be. I will focus on service, rather than volume. First Cheltenham will be nothing other than a local community bank, begun by a local banker.

Chapter 8

1994

After my meeting with Larsen and the drop of the injunction, I resolved to cut all ties, relinquishing all of my former responsibilities as director. I remained close with many of the Cheltenham employees, receiving my information primarily from word of mouth. By the spring of 1994, my cup was overflowing with other things, particularly Joan.

Joan was like a sister to me, but was a handful, especially during my last four years with Cheltenham. More and more, my office filing cabinets were being filled with Joan's various contracts or proposals of new adventures. Four years before the incident with Corestates, Joan found an outlet for her custom designed jewelry through QVC shopping network. A year after her QVC start, in addition to the still running *Joan Rivers Show*, she launched *Gossip! Gossip! Gossip!*, a weekly half-hour show on the USA Network. Both shows ran their course and were cancelled in 1993. Joan then tried a different format with *Can We Shop?*, a syndicated semi-version of home shopping, but it never took, forcing Joan to rely more on her continuing success with QVC.

When QVC first gave Joan the opportunity to design and sell her own line of costume jewelry, I offered my approval to duplicate a pin, given to her as a birthday present, two years before Edgar's death. After learning that the word "Melissa" represents the word "bee" in Greek, I had the gold and diamond bee pin custom made by Tony Fratone, my own local Hatboro jeweler, in honor of Joan's daughter. The duplication of the pin became one of her most profitable pieces, helping to launch the success of *The Joan Rivers Classic Collection*.

Joan's high profile and increasing sales matched well with QVC, until 1992, when Barry Diller, previously with Fox, joined the network. In a 6:00 a.m. phone call, Joan told me through hysterical tears about Diller's association. Fearing the loss of her QVC position, she was desperate for some kind of insurance policy that would lead to a more secure vantage point.

At that time, I had been working with a company called Regal Communications for two years. I was first introduced to Regal's head, Arthor Toll, while eating a slice of brochette in a local Maple Glenn pizzeria. Jerry Levinson, a community video store owner, approached me with the unknown Toll, telling me that Toll was interested in one of my *Two Ponds* homes. I had only known Levinson casually through my brother Joe, from whom he rented his store space. My brother vouched for Levinson as a respected businessman and in turn, Levinson made an equivalent voucher for Toll, so I pursued the sale.

Although Arthur Toll never bought the home, he contracted me for a new Regal building in Fort Washington. Before the building's construction, Toll told me of a stock requirement for all employees. Since he had only recently taken his business public, as a contractor, I would have to purchase Regal stock to illustrate an investment in the company's interest. Having dabbled in the stock market previously, I had no problems with Toll's request and continued to purchase 50,000 shares over the next four weeks.

Regal was a mass marketing corporation, selling anything from office to exercise equipment through extensive television infomercials. Bruce Edmonson, the chief financial officer for the corporation, previously worked with my secretary Helen's son. It was his voucher, as well, that allowed me to continue my relationship with Toll. I resumed handling big construction jobs and financed one of his buildings for a million dollars, securing the deal on a handshake alone. Although our business dealings were good, my relationship with Toll never exceeded the lines of business.

When Joan called, looking for a means to secure her QVC position, I had to think fast. On a previous visit to Pennsylvania, she had met Toll and his wife on separate occasions and liked them both. I thought of Toll and his influences in television, concluding that if Joan merged with Regal, it would supply a necessary buffer to Diller. Joan agreed, figuring that if she did lose her job with QVC, she would still have an outlet to sell her jewelry with Regal's guaranteed television time. By the end of 1992, Joan and her two partners cut a deal with Regal, earning Joan fourteen million dollars in stock and an extra half a million a year more than what she was making from QVC alone.

Only a year after their companies merged, Barry Diller left the shopping network, without ever causing any trouble for Joan. Joan and Toll hit it off well and continued with their business.

Soon, however, I began to take notice of certain discrepancies in Toll's character. I still trusted him enough as a businessman that I continued buying stock in his growing company, however, there was something hidden about him that I just could not put my finger on. It began when Toll started visiting my home with his daughter. She would bring "home-baked" cookies that I knew were store-bought. I found both the cookie incident and Toll's daughter to be as mysterious as Toll himself.

It was not long before the mystery was solved for me. At the start of 1994, Ernst & Young began an audit on Regal Communications, revealing two sets of books. Toll claimed to have about a hundred million more than the company's actual net worth. Essentially, he cooked the books, floating thirty-five million dollars in bond issues, based on phony sales. All of the stock was worthless and Regal was forced to declare bankruptcy, bringing Joan's company down with it.

That same year, charges were brought against representatives of the company. Jerry Levinson and Regal's in-house lawyer, Elliot Fisher, cooperated with the government in selling out Toll. Levinson got probation time, while Fisher had six months of house arrest. Arthur Toll and Bruce Edmonson earned four years in prison between them.

Despite the money Joan had made over the years, she was furious that I had introduced her to Toll. By 1994, Cheltenham had taken all my energy and I was still recovering from its loss. At the same time, Joan was on me to get back her business. I called her accountant, Michael Karlin, and put the matter into his hands. For Joan's sake, Karlin made a deal with the bondholders, buying their worthless bonds at decreased prices. With no personal liability, Joan regained one hundred percent of the company, minus the two partners.

I resolve that, one day, I will wallpaper my office bathroom with my 50,000 shares of worthless Regal stock, to represent the lesson that I was stubborn to learn. I have held many friends and associates in my life and pride myself on keen judgment of character. Most of the time, I was right. When I was wrong, I suffered severe consequences beyond the sacrifice of pride.

On May 18, 1994, I was called to appear in front of the U.S. Securities and Exchange Commission, or SEC, in relation to an ongoing investigation. The SEC protects investors and maintains the integrity of the securities markets. It requires public companies to disclose meaningful financial information and enforces the securities laws, in order to prevent securities fraud. My deposition was needed regarding an insider trading charge against Robert Hunter, director on the Cheltenham and INBC Boards, as well as a member of the Cheltenham Group.

Hunter, like the rest of the board members, had a fiduciary duty to both boards and to shareholders not to purchase INBC stock while in possession of "material, nonpublic information" concerning proposed mergers between INBC and any potential partners. As a member of the INBC Board, Hunter had been aware that Corestates was interested in a possible merger, yet he continued to buy stock through November. After buying the stock, he had told his girlfriend, her daughter, and several of his friends, including Kenneth Greenwood, another Cheltenham Group member, to purchase INBC stock.

As a fellow board member, I had been an acquaintance of Greenwood's for many years. When he was not at Cheltenham, he spent most of his hours running his father's family established furniture store. Over the years, I had been generous to Greenwood and his business, sending my friends and family to his store with their furniture needs. When I disassociated myself with the Cheltenham Group, I also disassociated myself personally from Greenwood. I had not seen him since the loss of Cheltenham. Although I never classified Greenwood as a great friend, I did place a certain faith in my judgment of his character. He seemed to be a hard working man with generally good intentions in life. With this in mind, I was surprised to be hearing of his illegal stock trading. Although Greenwood was not a member of the INBC Board, he apparently used the information offered by Hunter to purchase stock.

Hunter and I experienced our differences awhile back. However, I never particularly labeled him as one of the bad guys, not even after Long told me that Hunter had voted against my purchase proposal of INBC. My interview with John Hefferman, the SEC agent assigned, confirmed that, although Hunter may be a good guy, he certainly had bad judgment.

My subpoena from the SEC was standard procedure. They gathered their investigative facts from informal inquiry, interviewing witnesses, examining brokerage records, and reviewing trading data. I offered my full cooperation in answering the questions that pertained to both Greenwood and Hunter and dismissed the interview as the closing chapter in the Cheltenham story. I held no resentment toward Greenwood and Hunter. However, if they were in fact guilty, which the evidence did not necessarily imply, I would be on the same side as justice.

My sympathies were with Hunter, after hearing of the events that followed his investigation. I do not believe that Hunter ever had a chance at justice. He merely became the victim of a raw deal and a raw relationship.

Hunter's girlfriend, twenty-five years his junior, was also required to appear in front of John Hefferman. I warned Hunter five years before, when he took up with this New Jersey shore bartender, that the largest attraction between such a young girl and a sixty-some-year-old man was his money. But, there is no fool like an old fool and Hunter illustrated it fully. He spent some of his money supporting this woman and her thirteen-year-old daughter, buying their love through the lap of luxury.

The irony of life caught up with Hunter, when John Hefferman began seeing this woman. Hefferman and the girl were witnessed around town together, while Hunter's future remained largely in Hefferman's hands. If Hefferman's damage was not enough, he and the girl, in my opinion, devised a plot, putting Hunter out of commission permanently. Shortly after their affair began, the woman brought charges against Hunter for sexually molesting her daughter. When it was revealed that the daughter was a virgin, they dropped the case. Three weeks later, it was reopened. This time, she claimed that Hunter forced the daughter to perform oral sexual acts on him—an accusation hard to prove.

Unaware of what was happening to him and his relationship, Hunter hired a private investigator that got Hefferman and Hunter's former girlfriend together on tape. Publicly embarrassed, the SEC moved the insider trading case from Philadelphia to New York. Only weeks before the trial's conclusion, Hefferman married the Jersey girl. In the spring of 1995, after his second trial, Hunter was sentenced to fourteen years in prison for child molestation on top of his much smaller prison sentence for insider trading.

My compassion for Hunter brought me to his second trial as a character witness. I knew Hunter long enough to believe that his bad judgment could have led to insider trading, but I could not believe that he was guilty of sexual molestation. I had seen Hunter with the teenage girl, and witnessed nothing but genuine father-like affection. I had seen Hunter with my own children, and never doubted his good nature. Under oath, I testified in front of a jury to all of this. Sadly, it was in vain.

At the age of sixty-five, Hunter lost his liberties. Three months after Hunter began his sentence, the former girlfriend offered to withdraw the charges for seven hundred thousand dollars. Although the woman was willing to sacrifice her daughter's reputation for some cash, Hunter refused to sacrifice his innocence. The woman left Hefferman and left town, shortly after.

I had been surrounded by too many frauds in too short a period of time. I had no intentions of being associated with such recurring characters and their blatant flaws. With my reputation still in tact, I focused on building and harbored any bank business beyond the normal customer/institution relationship. At the time, 1994 was shelved as the most horrendous year of my life. I could not have known that the worst was yet to come.

After my experiences with Maria, Larsen, and Toll, one would imagine that I would reserve more prudence in my relations. I thought that I had. Now, I realize that a den of thieves would follow me, gradually stripping me of all that I hold dear.

Chapter 9

PHILLY LAND

After the last drawn out years, I looked forward to changing my lifestyle. My first grandchild had just been born, and with a grandfather's pride, I made myself more available to the family. Career wise, I resumed building with a clean slate. I handled any news of Cheltenham as a distant onlooker, offering only a sympathetic ear. It was 1995 and I put the past far behind, focusing on a fresh future. At the end of January, my good friend and reliable associate, Alan Goldman, called on behalf of the Philadelphia Mayor, Ed Rendell, with a building proposal that would redirect my energies.

Alan Goldman and Ed Rendell engaged in preliminary discussions concerning the development of the Philadelphia Naval Yard. The Philadelphia Naval Yard was twelve hundred acres of land located at the convergence of the Schuylkill and Delaware rivers. Established in 1868, it had been a site for Naval shipbuilding, repair, and maintenance, as well as an important contribution to the city's economic well being. The announced closing of the Naval Base in 1993 signaled the continued erosion of Philadelphia as a financial and commercial center.

With the Base remaining dormant over the previous two years, Alan called to trigger my interest as developer, and secured a meeting with Rendell, Alan, and myself. I had met Alan over twenty years previous through my brother Frankie. Since then, Alan and I shared a close friendship, along with many business and charitable opportunities. This particular opportunity would be allowing us to combine the two. I trusted Alan with my life, but had my reservations about Rendell.

I never voted for Rendell as Mayor, since I had developed my distrust for him when he ran for District Attorney. Rendell looked to secure the District Attorney votes in a clean and speedy trial for the murder of Greek mob leader, Steve Boris, who had been shot in a local Philadelphia restaurant. The clean and speedy trial resulted in the conviction of an innocent man, Neil Farber, the nephew of my good friend and land broker, Jack Gervertz. Farber served seven years on death row, until his innocence was finally proven in court. The four million dollars that Farber was granted in a suit against the city after his release meant little in light of his deteriorated mental state, which resulted from prison. I would be naive to blame Rendell solely for Farber's tragic situation. However, I have developed a general distrust for any person that would sacrifice an innocent life for his own career advancement.

When Rendell secured the role of Mayor, I again attempted to put the past behind, optimistic of potential Philadelphia employment and tax reform. Crossing paths with Rendell at several fundraisers, I even contributed to his Democratic party, despite my Republican roots. It was not until Rendell inappropriately solicited funds at a mutual friend's funeral that I began to re-evaluate his sincerity.

Although I had my own issues with Rendell, I agreed to meet with him for Alan's sake, figuring that his public persona offered a certain security to any business propositions. I canceled some church affairs to meet Rendell and Alan on a relaxed Sunday at City Hall. At our meeting, the Mayor told me of his interest in developing the east end of the Philadelphia Naval Yard. He gave me and Alan until the end of March to come up with a development plan and appropriate financing that would be beneficial to the city. I agreed on the condition that the project would be charitable and a joint effort between the city of Philadelphia and our development group.

By the end of the meeting, it was agreed that the federal government would supply the land, while we would come up with financing from bond issues. Our intention was to take half of the development's profits to the city of Philadelphia and half to surrounding charitable organizations, ensuring that Rendell would not personally profit from the deal. At lunch with Alan later that day, I roughly scribbled out a business plan, blueprints, and a scale model on some napkins for what we would call *Philly Land*.

Alan and I set out the first steps toward the creation of a world-class business complex that would provide the city with a proper return for an asset with tremendous potential for growth. To realize the full potential of the site and its location, *Philly Land* was conceived as a blended mixture of retail, entertainment, public service, cultural activities, and selective manufacturing. The balance was assumed to provide the best economic returns in the form of jobs and in the creation of capital for the city of Philadelphia.

With the addition of Joe Wise, a naval architect and marine engineer, we continued to form the Philadelphia International Development Group (PIDG), appointing each member with the following responsibilities: Alan with public relations and community affairs, Joe with engineering, and myself with building and finance. Together, we ironed out the details and proposed our joint venture with the city of Philadelphia to develop, own, and operate this multi-faceted complex. At the beginning of March, Rendell received our proposal, which consisted of market analysis, redevelopment vision, financial planning, and management credentials.

Within our vision, we saw the integrated set of structures built on a single foundation. The all-enclosed, year-round Amusement Park would be set on seventy-five acres, directly adjacent to the United Nations Theme Park. Entertainment City would consist of five motion picture studios, a five-thousand-seat theatre, and a three-story radio and television center. The International Trade Center would offer trade show space, as well as a shipping and receiving area. A one million square foot factory outlet mall would house four major retail stores. The twenty-six-screen cinema complex would seat one hundred fifty people per screening. We proposed three hotels, each consisting of six hundred rooms, in accordance with the projected growth in the business and leisure markets. The manufacturing market would be extensive, including modular housing, sporting goods, furniture and textiles. The Sports Hall of Fame would comprise part of the Cultural Activities, as would the Arts and Science Center, The Navy Yard Museum, and The Eighteenth Century Historic Sea Port Village.

PIDG prepared and submitted, along with our proposal, a formal and detailed business plan, site plan, and scale model of *Philly Land*, which fully described the project and its benefits to Philadelphia. We planned the total construction in two phases of two years each. The construction itself would create approximately three thousand jobs. An additional thirteen to fourteen thousand permanent jobs would be created for its full operation.

Philly Land would be financed wholly with private funds, requiring no capital from Philadelphia, only tax abatements in the start up years as development incentive. It was estimated to be a seven- billion-dollar asset for the city, generating seven to eight hundred million in yearly profits after the debt was paid. Market assumptions based on census information and other government data published by the U.S. Chamber of Commerce allowed us to predict that the project's entire debt would be paid off in its first six years of business. With the debt extinguished, all *Philly Land* profits would be distributed evenly between the city of Philadelphia and charitable causes, rendering it the biggest charity in the history of Pennsylvania.

After reviewing our proposal, Rendell wrote me a letter of response on March 13, saying, "I'm very impressed with your vision and obvious enthusiasm for developing the site." He also stated that he was impressed with our plan to distribute the proceeds, which demonstrated our "spirit of dedication and civic-mindedness that is all too rare these days." Rendell concluded the letter, "If anyone can pull this project off, I know it is you and your group."

At our next meeting, held only six days after the date of the letter, Rendell said the project was a "grand slam home run in the bottom of the ninth." He continued to encourage PIDG's development of the Navy Base, appointing his Deputy Mayor, Mark Gaige, to work closely with us in the realization of *Philly Land*. Rendell committed himself, as the Mayor of Philadelphia, to formally naming PIDG developers in the fall, provided that we maintain a comprehensive business plan supporting the viability of *Philly Land*; demonstrate and support the major companies willing to participate in Philly Land; and demonstrate more fully our financial strength to accomplish the project. Certainly, all were reasonable requests considering the grandeur of our vision.

We proceeded, based on Rendell's word, to acquire support and commitment from worthy individuals and corporations. By the first of August, Hopper Soliday had agreed to serve as our investment banking firm, underwriting and placing up to two billion dollars of "tax exempt facility revenue bonds to fund the cost of construction and operation of *Philly Land*." Shortly after, we received letters of interest from MGM in relation to Entertainment City, from Pepsi Cola in relation to the Amusement Park, from Regal in relation to the Cinema Complex, and from Holiday Inn and Marriot in relation to the hotels. Alan and I had combined our resources in obtaining a two-hundred-million dollar line of credit. By fall, we had commitments to seventy percent of the leasing property and eighty percent of bond sales, all before any steps were taken to break ground.

Mark Gaige was as dedicated to *Philly Land* as was PDIG. Gaige wrote a letter to Alan Cole-Ford, Executive Vice President of Strategy and Development for MGM, reaffirming the city's interest in working with MGM and extending an invitation to tour the base at their convenience. However, when MGM presented their timeframe for the tour, other city officials denied their requests. And, toward the end of October, Rendell still had not formally named us developer.

I continued to maintain an ongoing correspondence with Rendell, updating him on our progress and enthusiasm. I then received from Rendell an unusually formal letter, in which he stated that my "proposal for *Philly Land* is potentially interesting, however, we are currently considering several projects at the Navy Base."

Rendell was up to something. Other projects had never been mentioned before, but soon, they filtered through the papers, particularly in the names of German shipbuilder Meyer Werft and ship repair specialist Metro Machine Inc.

Our "grand slam" was now reevaluated as only "potentially interesting." I invested two hundred thousand dollars into this proposal, only for Rendell to undermine it as a mere product of brainstorming, whimsically introduced and void of any preparation. The only thing that I found void was Rendell's integrity. The money that I invested was not an issue. The project was intended to benefit the community, not the financial advancement of individuals. I had my success and this was my opportunity to give something big back. Apparently, Rendell saw things differently. My assumption that we had not offered Rendell enough pocket change may have been correct, because the campaign over *Philly Land* continued into the spring of 1996. The last few years taught me a lesson about chasing after old horses. I submitted my arguments for *Philly Land*'s value and left the decision to the city. Alan was not as easily deterred. He continued barking through April of 1996, as I continued on a new adventure.

In February, I took a much-needed vacation in Florida with my daughter, son-in-law, and granddaughter, Krista. I was eager to relax and escape the growing hostility with the Mayor over the city's future. One evening, while driving along the Florida coast with Krista, she drew my attention to the "pretty castles," pointing to the ornamentally lit buildings that dressed the shoreline. I asked her if she wanted Poppy to build her a castle of her own. The restlessness of Florida's relaxation soon gave birth to *Krista's Kastle, Oceanside Resort and Hotel*.

On March 29, after a month-long property search, the final settlement took place for my purchase of the former Quality Inn in Pompano Beach, Florida. With a crew of seventy men, I began to gut the entire nine-story hotel, initializing the first stages of Kastle construction. The crew worked around the clock refurbishing the hotel, while I flew frequent commutes from Florida to Pennsylvania. The welcomed challenge of erecting my granddaughter's castle as a hotel was enough to distract me from *Philly Land*, until reading an April 11 newspaper article in *The South Philadelphia Review*. I was passing time on a return flight to Philadelphia when I read a quote from the Mayor, in response to mine and Alan's proposal of *Philly Land*: "The bottom line here is that they are homebuilders with a grandiose idea, but they don't have two nickels to back it up."

Initially, I was amused, mostly at my perception of the Mayor's apparent ignorance. I did not bother fishing my pockets for proof of two nickels. I had mistaken my two hundred million in credit to be suitable enough. As far as our idea, it was certainly grandiose, but well designed and planned in every aspect of its construction. My track record in the building business had surely taken me beyond the label of "homebuilder," and with it came the reputation that led Rendell to approach me in the first place.

With each reread of the article, my amusement gradually gave way to general resentment. Mark Gaige was now former Deputy Mayor, just previously relieved of his position while voicing support for *Philly Land*. He was quoted in the same article as saying, "Tommy and Alan are two of the most honest and honorable people I've ever seen in the business and that's rare in 1996." I realized with Gaige's quote that Rendell was not only portraying his ignorance to our idea, but also questioning our honor.

Dated April 11, I wrote my own letter of response to Rendell, while still enjoying the flight home. It was published as a full page in the May 23 issue of *The South Philadelphia Review*:

Mayor Rendell,

You are quoted in the April 11, 1996 edition of the *South Philadelphia Review* as stating, **"The bottom line here is that they are home builders with a grandiose idea, but they don't have two nickels to back it up."** Please find enclosed five nickels—two bits—for the value of your word and commitments. You need it more that I do. But it is not money that makes the man, but his deeds. This may help to explain why you cannot fathom the value and growing support for the *Philly Land* project. *Philly Land* is about sharing and giving to less fortunate individuals, aided by others who transform their words into deeds. How to do this profitably, while providing good paying jobs with benefits and donating these profits to charity, may seem "too good to be true" by some.

Speaking as someone who has been successful without the need and support of taxpayers' money, I can understand why the concept may be difficult for those who benefit at the expense of toiling taxpayers.

Although we do have a firm grasp as to what may have happened to cause your reversal [of commitment], we do listen carefully to your comments and have wondered about your public endorsements.

From here on, you should be careful that you do not incorrectly discuss my abilities and character. Since we first shared our $7 billion *Philly Land* development with you. I have continually and actively been solicited for my financial support for your personal agenda. Please reread my reply to Alan Kessler to refresh your memory. Your agenda has been for Ed Rendell and feathering your own nest. Our agenda, unlike yours, and the business records of *Philly Land* will be open. This is my word and supported by my deeds.

P.S. My creed in life is honor, integrity, and commitments. On a scale of 1-10, I place you at a negative number: -0.

———◆———

I have always refused to be a "yes" man, speaking my peace at any cost. It has been labeled both my best and worst quality. No doubt, Rendell found it to be my worst, when he faced a public undressing that exposed his most horrible side. After this letter's publication, I filed it with the rest of my "love" letters from Rendell. We terminated any future correspondence and fastened to a mutual disdain.

Shortly after, he gave the Anglo-Norwegian firm Kvaerner approximately four hundred eighty million dollars in subsidies to build up the base, for which Kvaerner was obligated to create between seven hundred and one thousand jobs. It was rumored that of the subsidies, eighty million came from the city of Philadelphia, one hundred million from the state of Pennsylvania, and three hundred million from the federal government. Kvaerner, faced with low-cost competition from other countries, soon withdrew from the shipbuilding business and declared bankruptcy. I believe that Rendell received a hefty donation to his Democratic Party and personal agenda, while taxpayers paid royally for virtually nothing. The Philadelphia Naval Yard remains dormant to this day.

I gave up on Mayor Ed Rendell, but not on the idea of *Philly Land*. Today, the business proposal remains locked away in a filing cabinet; the blueprints rest deskside among piled-high papers and rolls of building plans; and the scale model sits proudly at my office entrance within First Cheltenham Financial.

*Scale model of **Philly Land**, which sits proudly at the author's office entrance at First Cheltenham Financial.*

Chapter 10

THE TRIAL

I continued to hear rumors of Rendell's huffing and puffing after the publication of my letter. Unaffected, I left Rendell in Philadelphia, placing all of my attention toward Florida and the completion of *Krista's Kastle*. The one hundred-room hotel was becoming a castle in my own eyes, as I absorbed its multi-million-dollar view, overlooking miles of Pompano Beach front. Birthed through my granddaughter's words and my own imagination, *Krista's Kastle* was nurtured into reality. With tiki, patio, and lounge bars, a state of the art nightclub, a four-star restaurant, a more casual poolside barbeque, and the Joan Rivers Penthouse Suite, we held our ceremonial ribbon cutting. After finishing a big Fourth of July celebration open to the public, I began to plan for the hotel's official upcoming opening.

My plans suffered a brief interruption from the SEC, who requested another deposition in the investigation of insider trading. Cheltenham was becoming a bad cold, a lingering germ that I could not fully shake. With Bob Hunter already tried and convicted, I assumed this particular deposition would cater to Ken Greenwood. It had been two years since my last deposition. At that time, I was under the impression that Greenwood had pleaded guilty, although I had not yet received any word on his legal proceedings. Shortly after the first round of SEC hearings, Greenwood had sold the family furniture business, the business that his father had built from scratch. Since then, I had not given Greenwood another thought.

It seemed unusual that the SEC would continue to interview regarding events that took place almost three years earlier. I knew that Greenwood was being charged with three counts of insider trading, first in January 1994, during a quiet period, and again in October and November of the same year with knowledge of the pending merger. I had no problems in assisting the SEC through my deposition. The last SEC interview had been brief and painless, supplying honest answers to general questions about Cheltenham meetings and their agenda. I did my civil duty and left the site of *Krista's Kastle* for a July interview with the Securities & Exchange Commission.

The meeting was scheduled as one of many errands that day and approached with the same confidence of a quickly resolved task. Shortly into the meeting, my confidence was extinguished by the course dampness of Audry Weintrob, the SEC agent responsible for the interview. Ms. Weintrob was harshly rough in both appearance and personality, with a face that haunted men's memories longer than they liked. I endured hours of repeated questions, most of them intended to lead me astray. Weintrob lacked the general inquisitive tone of Hefferman years before. Instead, her voice was often laced with accusation, as she repeatedly asked questions to which I could have no answers. She inquired to discussions held within the confines of the INBC board-room. When I reminded her that I was not on that board, Ms. Weintrob temporarily dismissed the questions, only to disguise them later through attempted veiled words and contexts.

I left the interview mentally exhausted and torn between feelings of disappointment and relief. I was disappointed that my interview seemed unproductive in the investigative process and relieved that my ignorance would possibly conclude my involvement with the SEC. Ms. Weintrob left an uneasiness that, for the time, remained a mystery. I returned to Florida, hoping to never encounter her again.

Krista's Kastle became my most gratifying project. It seemed my only touch of gold that had not turned into dust over the past few years of my life. The hotel formally opened in September with a guest appearance by Joan Rivers. With the hire of a competent general manager, my Florida visits were not needed as often. At fifty-one years old and with the promise of more grandchildren, I put my adventures behind me and welcomed the low profile of local building.

In November 1996, I received a certified letter, stating that I was the target for a grand jury investigation of insider trading. The target letter came from the desk of the United States Attorney, Michael R. Stiles, ironically, the neighbor and friend of Mayor Ed Rendell. My attorney looked into the letter, assuring me that it was nonsense without any legal base. My contacts in the FBI also diminished the letter's severity, verifying that they were unaware of any investigation. I dismissed it as well, attributing it to an outlet for Rendell to flex his political muscles. Rendell had definitely won the round.

Exactly one year later, in November 1997, I was indicted for insider trading, referring back four years to my attempted purchase of Cheltenham. On May 26, 1998, I went to trial in front of the Honorable Eduardo Robreno, defending myself against the United States of America on four counts of insider trading and two counts of wire fraud. The four counts of insider trading included the two stock purchases made on November 1, one purchase on November 4, and the final stock purchase on November 17. The wire fraud was a bonus, claiming that since the money was wired to my broker, it was illegal. If it were mailed, I would have been charged with mail fraud. If I had delivered the money personally, fraud would have never been an issue. I went to trial with little fear and a lot of trust in the justice system. How they could have even fathomed the charge when all my stock was *sold* with the knowledge of the bank's merger, I did not know.

My defense lawyer, Tom Bergstrom, was hired on poor advise from my real estate lawyer. The prosecutor was assistant U.S. Attorney, Joe Poluka, who I believe was taking his orders directly from Stiles. The basis of the trial revolved around confidential INBC meetings with Corestates, beginning in September 1993, and orchestrated mostly through Monroe Long and John Harding. The prosecutor seemed to find it irrelevant that I was neither a board member of INBC, nor a participant of any mentioned meetings.

Poluka clung to the false statement that I attended the November 1 meeting with the Cheltenham Group, attempting to prove that merger discussions were integrated as an essential part of the group's agenda. I had neither attended that meeting, nor was it my understanding that the merger was discussed. If Poluka could prove that I had previous knowledge of the merger's material and nonpublic information, which I did not, then my stock purchases were seen as a scheme to defraud the shareholders of INBC in connection with insider trading. Since the financial support for my purchases were wired, wire fraud was viewed as the execution of this scheme.

The trial reintroduced the faded memories and characters of my Cheltenham days, all offering testimony in support or defense of my attendance at the November 1 meeting. According to Poluka, it was to be the determining factor to the court's verdict. Poluka's case relied on his star witness, Kenneth Greenwood. Coincidentally, Greenwood had not yet received his own sentencing, despite his previous admission of guilt to insider trading in front of a Federal judge. He had struck a deal. Apparently, this deal included offering false testimony against me.

I was offered my own deal just before the trial. In March, Bergstrom and Poluka drew up an agreement without my knowledge. Essentially, it was a plea bargain, swapping prison time for a large sum of money and an admission of guilt. Bergstrom obviously wanted his check without the inconvenience of a trial. I refused. Innocent men do not make bargains. Neither man accounted for my self-respect and the invaluable price of my honor, integrity, and name.

Shortly after, Poluka pulled my sister Rosemary aside, seeking to meet with me "informally" and alone, void of legal representation. Suspicious of his unorthodox request and his intentions, I again refused. Poluka was a smooth talker, and I had no doubt that he was a dirty player, skilled at manipulating words to his own benefit. If I met privately with him, I would be placing myself on the battlefield without ammunition. Poluka was a skinny, awkward looking fellow, who reminded me of the kid in every high school who had trouble making friends. As an adult lawyer, I found him eager to misuse the power that he probably lacked in his youth. Poluka's request for a meeting confirmed my suspicions that he had a weak case against me. He, too, wanted to avoid a trial. With a renewed faith in the "good guy," I had no fear. I welcomed the trial and the opportunity to clear my smeared name.

Greenwood took the stand early in the trial, with paling cheeks under the visible glisten of sweat accumulation. His lips were tremulous as he squeezed out stammered words in response to Poluka's questions. With his eyes fixed on the floor, Greenwood testified to a specific recollection of me at the November 1 meeting, along with a specific recollection of merger discussions. From that point on, his testimony was all over the place, pingponging throughout the courtroom. At his SEC interview back in May 1994, he made a deposition under oath, stating he did not feel comfortable testifying that I had attended the meeting. He also testified that there were no discussions of the pending merger. In his 1996 SEC testimony, he stated he would be guessing to say that I had attended that meeting, because he did not have any recollection. Yet, taking the stand at my trial in 1997, Greenwood made no mistake of placing me in the Cheltenham Boardroom for the November 1 meeting.

When cross-examined, Greenwood said that he was confused during both SEC interviews. He claimed to be "unprepared," "under mental stress," and "mixed up mentally." How can you be "unprepared" to tell the truth? Greenwood claimed that he was now more prepared to look over his testimony and make corrections. He was now, four years later, more prepared to tell the truth, more prepared than he had been six months after the incident at his first SEC interview. When asked how he could be so sure now, Greenwood said that he had time to "review the facts." Only moments later, he admitted that reviewing the facts meant reviewing other people's testimonies, which is an obstruction of justice in itself.

Greenwood also testified that he was unaware of my intentions on buying Cheltenham. Again contradicting himself, he later mentioned a June 1993 meeting in which my intended purchase of Cheltenham was discussed. Greenwood's testimony did not have an impact on my optimism. He put his own lacking character on display with his questionable body language and obvious "mental stress."

After the trial, I found out the details behind Greenwood's deal. Greenwood had traded stock during a silent period in January. However, his guilt stemmed from ignorance, not intent, since he was unaware of the silent period at the time. He was offered forgiveness for his January offense, if he pleaded guilty to the other two offenses. Apparently, he had bought and traded stock in October and November 1993, with the knowledge of a merger. He pleaded guilty to those two charges, when promised only a slap on the wrist. Essentially, the SEC was looking to hang us all.

By having Greenwood plead guilty to the October and November counts, they attempted to place him in the same time period as me. They were looking to trade a body for a body. Greenwood got his slap on the wrist, only five years probation with thirty-six hundred hours of community service. Greenwood could not have handled prison. He was a weak man, sacrificing an innocent future through government-approved lies, in an attempt to buy his own freedom. Greenwood may not have gone to prison, but he will never be free.

At the trial, I watched as ghosts of Cheltenham took turns at the witness stand. Mickey Schrenk testified, as previously in his SEC interviews, that I was not at the November 1 meeting, nor was the Corestates merger mentioned. My absence was specifically recalled because he had telephoned my secretary Helen just before the meeting's start, inquiring of my whereabouts.

Harry Barbin remained consistent in his previous SEC deposition, stating that he could "not verify" I was there, because he was not sure, and he had never spoken to me personally about the meeting, only left a message at my office. Barbin also claimed that he did not "specifically recall" any mention of the Corestates merger, certain that his own knowledge of the merger was not revealed.

Fred Dreher told the court that it was his "strong recollection," now and at the initial SEC interview, that I "was not present" at the November 1 meeting. Dreher's former assistant, Mary Mullany had testified twice in the past, and again at my trial, that I had not been present at the November 11 meeting, but had been present at the November 1 meeting, obviously confusing her dates, because there had been no question to my attendance on the November 11 meeting. As note-taker for the meeting, Mullany could not find evidence in her own writing that placed me at the first meeting in question. Each witness, with the exception of Greenwood, confirmed my absence at the November 1 meeting, not only at this present trial, but also at SEC interviews in the past. Poluka's accusation that I received privileged merger information at that meeting was becoming unsubstantiated.

Although Monroe Long could only confirm receiving my phone call before the meeting, he did testify that I had never attended an INBC meeting in the year of 1993, nor did he ever mention to me the meetings with Terry Larsen concerning the merger. While on the stand, Monroe acknowledged his first offer from Larsen was on September 27, just before the INBC Board meeting that had supposedly unanimously voted down my own purchase of Cheltenham. He also revealed that the Cheltenham Group members on that board had not actually voted me down, but rather had abstained from voting. They had abstained due to their conflict of interest, redeeming them from the turncoat label that I had assigned.

If I had known this in November of 1993, I would have never disassociated myself from the group or its meetings. Without a doubt, I would have attended the November 1 meeting, refraining from the purchase of stock until a group decision was made. Ultimately, I would never have been subjected to this ugly mess or accused of such a heinous crime. Monroe had divided me from the Cheltenham Group, perhaps unintentionally, but still successfully. He weakened our efforts, at the same time strengthening his opportunities in the Corestates merger.

As the trial proceeded, I began to see my present effort weakening as well, particularly with the realization of my own attorney's incompetence, illustrated clearly through his wife's dominating role in his personal decisions and in the courtroom. Bergstrom's wife attended each day of the trial, offering too many of her own opinions on whom he should call to the stand and when. Upon his wife's suggestion, Bergstrom found it unnecessary for Joan Rivers to testify as a strong character witness, claiming it would turn the trial into a media playpen. He also opted against former FBI agent, Dick Ritter, taking the stand. Ritter was aware of my Cheltenham involvement since the David Astheimer incident and could have testified to my intentions of buying the bank.

Through the majority of the trial, Bergstrom even insisted there was no need for me to take the stand to defend myself. He assured me that the evidence in my favor would speak for itself. I watched day after day as Poluka called his plethora of witnesses to the stand and Bergstrom received them all with weak cross-examinations, failing to ask the pertinent questions that would prove my innocence.

Poluka called Terry Larsen to the stand, questioning our involvement. Larsen testified that he vaguely remembered meeting me in his office and could not even remember what bank I represented, failing to mention any of his promises or my offers. Denying the presence of Jim Carnie, Larsen also testified to meeting me alone. If my own attorney were skilled, he would have called Jim Carnie to the stand to testify to what Larsen claimed not to remember. Carnie's presence would have immediately placed question to Larsen's integrity, and supported my honest intentions of buying the bank, at the same time diminishing any perceived intentions of fraud.

Charles Sielski, the Philadelphia Postal Inspector, was called to the stand, testifying that my money was wired, which it was. The postal inspector could prove that I wired money for the purchase of INBC stock from my Cheltenham account to my broker's firm, R.W. Baird in Wisconsin. I had never denied it. What Sielski could not prove was my intentions for purchasing that stock. Without the intent to defraud, there was no fraud in wiring money. It is a standard practice in the purchase of any stock. My lawyer never bothered to question the relevance of Sielski's testimony. To a juror uneducated in the stock exchange, it looked like the introduction of new incriminating evidence, when it was merely a review of standard procedure.

Poluka's most potent move was the introduction of Robert Kaplan, a registered broker dealer in securities. Kaplin took the stand as a specialist, examining the stock records of my nephew John. John had purchased four hundred shares of INBC stock on November 17,

1993. My brother Joe's records indicated a ten thousand-share purchase of the same stock on November 18, the same day as the INBC press release. Poluka was attempting to prove that their purchases were made on my suggestion, a suggestion that insinuated previous knowledge of the merger. Before the trial, I had been unaware of either's stock history, and myself deemed it a curiously odd coincidence.

My INBC stock purchases were made with the sole intention of buying Cheltenham. Tipping off anyone to buy INBC stock would have only been detrimental to my cause. With an increase of purchased stock, there is an increase per share price, which would have made my own attempt more costly. The testimony of John and Joe, as I found out later, would have revealed their ignorance to my Cheltenham position and the solicitations made by our shared broker, Michael Acampora, to purchase the stock. The judge reminded the jury that my criminal charges did not concern the stock purchases of family members. Rather, the stock histories were admitted only for the limited purpose of deciding the extent of my material and nonpublic information. Since the histories were introduced, I viewed it an integral part of the case. Without hearing Joe and John's testimony, the semblance of guilt was introduced to the courtroom, perhaps not in the original form, but through my implied role in their purchases. Neither relative was ever called to the stand. Instead, Michael Acampora was.

Acampora divulged our seven-year history together, detailing his assumption of my past stock objectives, including INBC. Acampora, never aware of my intentions of buying Cheltenham, offered only my tendency at strategic accumulation, resulting in short term profits. However, he did testify to my sale of stock on November 19, just before the potential profits that had accompanied the formal announcement of the Corestates merger.

Bergstrom asked general questions on the solicitation of stock orders, which were suggestions from the broker on specifically recommended or researched stock. Acampora included that INBC was a takeover candidate. It had been a popular recommendation at that time, and Acampora confirmed that the likelihood of a merger was apparent and, therefore, public information. Bergstrom failed to ask and Acampora failed to offer that he had been the direct broker of both John and Joe and that he had violated my confidentiality when soliciting the two to buy the stock in question. Bergstrom's whole examination relied on insinuations, rather than concrete confirmations from Acampora. Acampora, concerned strictly for commissions, answered only the questions asked.

After Acampora's cross-examination, it was fully apparent that Poluka would introduce anything possible to discredit my reputation. On the other hand, my lawyer, Bergstrom, displayed more concern over his wife's appeasement, than the pending verdict of the trial. So much so, that I began to wonder whose side he was really on. Despite Bergstrom's discouragement, I insisted that I take the stand, recognizing my own testimony as my best defense. If I could illustrate my Cheltenham battle to the jury, they would surely recognize my innocent intentions to purchase stock, consequently dismissing any notion of fraud.

I took the stand during the concluding days of the trial, detailing every aspect of Cheltenham from start to finish. I included the conviction of David Astheimer, my initial resignation, Monroe's request for my return, every stock purchase made with each specific intention, my proposal to Harding and its denial, my detailed whereabouts on November 1, my final sale of INBC stock, the injunction, the agenda and result of my meeting with Larsen, and everything in-between. I spoke quickly and confidently, and perhaps even excessively. Although often interrupted by each examining attorney, I felt the relief of a seven-day verbal constipation. I fought all time restraints, desperate to account for any relevance previously excluded from the trial.

I exuberated a new confidence at trial's end, feeling my testimony was a final resolution of truth, a final resolution to the battle and my reputation. I listened to each attorney's closing argument with a passive ear, as they summed up eight days of evidence. Poluka's swelling reliance on Greenwood's testimony and deductions of falsehoods from untruths left me unaffected. I admit to only a small sting when he closed his argument with a lie. He referred to Acampora as my exclusive broker, escalating the doubt of coincidence in John and Joe's purchase of INBC stock. Judge Robreno's charge to the court had put me more at ease. He informed the jury that stock purchases, other than my own, were introduced only as a determining factor concerning merger information, and that the purchases themselves were unrelated to any criminal charge brought against me.

Robreno reminded the court of Greenwoods own plea of guilt, saying they "should consider Mr. Greenwood's testimony with more caution than the testimony of other witnesses." He also warned, "the testimony of a witness may be discredited by showing that a witness testified falsely" or inconsistently through various testimonies. Robreno continued to supply the jurors with questions to consider. Did the witness impress you as honest? Did the witness have a particular reason not to tell the truth? Did the witness have a personal outcome in the case? Did the witness have a relationship with either the government or the defendant? Did the witness seem to have a good memory? Did the witness' testimony differ from the testimony of other witnesses?

All of these questions blatantly discredited Green-wood. He was the only Cheltenham employee to testify against me, and answering these questions gives unde-niable doubt to the integrity of his character. With Greenwood out of the way, all remaining evidence proved that I did not attend the November 1 meeting. For a guilty verdict, the jury must be convinced, beyond a reasonable doubt of two things. First, they must be convinced that I had access to the material and non-public merger information. Greenwood had claimed to receive his information at the November 1 meeting. Since I did not attend that meeting, I had no access to the information. Second, they must be convinced that I had participated in a scheme to defraud knowingly, willfully, and with the intention to defraud. My sale be-fore the formal merger announcement illustrated that I had no intentions of making a profit at the sharehold-ers expense. I was fully confident, after the depth of my testimony, that the purity of my intentions had been made clear. My purchase of INBC stock was for the wholly independent altruistic reason of purchasing Cheltenham, not to cheat, defraud, or trade on inside information.

Unfortunately, my confidence was only partially founded. The jury returned with their verdict, finding me guilty on one count of insider trading and one count of mail fraud. They admittedly rejected the government's argument, the government's evidence, and the gov-ernment's theory. With my absence at the November 1 meeting established, the jury dismissed the three in-sider trading charges associated with November 3 and 4. However, in accordance with Poluka, they failed to find the INBC stock purchase of my relatives to be merely coincidental. Of course the purchases were not coincidental, instead a solicitation from our shared broker. After Bergstrom failed to make that clear in court, the jury concluded, that between the group meeting on November 11 and the board meeting on November 18, I must have received that material nonpublic merger information and utilized it, not only for my own benefit, but also for the benefit of my family. The uncharged conduct of my relatives became a preponderance of evidence, increasing the severity of my charge and the severity of my pending sentence.

When it came time for Judge Robreno to address the court, he clung to a misinterpreted statement that I had made during my testimony. I had said that this was not a crime, but a mess, referring to the unfortunate circumstances suffered by an innocent man. I was not guilty; therefore, there was no crime. Before issuing my sentence, Robreno stated, "a mess is a bad business deal...this is something different and I don't find the defendant had displayed real remorse or contrition for having committed this crime." How could I be remorseful of a crime never committed? I would not make contrition to a priest for an uncommitted sin. The trial was becoming an endless circle with me lost in its dark center.

Robreno continued to address the court, with each word driving the blood from my cheeks. "Simply to slap him on the wrist and send Mr. Pileggi home would send the wrong message," he said. "And the message in our society is sent, particularly to a defendant to whom money is not any significant problem, by taking away the one thing that money can't buy—and that is his liberty." As he completed the utterance, I have no doubt that my jaw hit the table. However, that is not where I felt my pain. I felt the pain go past my heart and deep into my soul. This was not just about me going to prison. It was about the justice system going wrong. It was about the bad guys, like Rendell and Larsen, winning.

The Judge asked me to stand. The page of life that spread out before me resembled a movie in which I was its tragic star. "It is the judgment of the Court that the defendant, Thomas Pileggi, is hereby committed to the custody of the Bureau of Prisons to be imprisoned for a term of twenty one months," he said. It felt like the conclusion of a battle far beyond Cheltenham. It was a battle of good versus evil; a battle of truth versus deceit. I lost more than my freedom or my faith. I lost the name and reputation that I had worked so hard to preserve.

The entirety of the sentence included my self-surrender on a designated date to a specified institution within the Bureau of Prisons. When released from prison, I would be placed under supervision for a term of two years, spending three months in a halfway house and the remainder on probation. Thought of an appeal offered consolation enough for a dignified exit from the courtroom.

Bergstrom was responsible for the appeal and failed at his last chance of competence, his last chance of redemption. The submitted appeal included the full testimony of every witness, except mine. Bergstrom failed to insert the most powerful portion of my testimony, my starting ground with Cheltenham. Instead, he began mid-battle with my statement, "I could take over Cheltenham, because I would have tremendous power to do so." He portrayed me as an egotist and a conqueror, failing to include the significance of the statement's context. The statement was merely illustrating the necessary stock purchases to acquire Cheltenham. Yet, as submitted, someone would antici-pate the haunting laughter of a mad scientist to follow.

Bergstrom also submitted Poluka's closing argument, but not his own. The judge received only Poluka's summation of the entire trial, with little reminder of my own defense. When I confronted Bergstrom on his error, he blamed his secretary. When I confronted her, she quit her seventeen-year job; disgusted Bergstrom would illegitimately render her scapegoat. I proceeded to hire another attorney to resubmit my appeal. Since Bergstrom had procrastinated on the first submission for almost a year, it was too late. The appeal was denied.

By October 1999, I received an affidavit from Michael Acampora, taking responsibility for the solicitation of my brother's stock. Acampora not only admitted to soliciting the stock, but also to revealing all of my previous stock purchases. He had told my brother that I had bought the INBC stock, that the stock was acting like a takeover, and that the trading volume was very heavy. As a result, my brother placed his order for the stock purchase.

With Acampora's confession and the likelihood of prison realized, I addressed Judge Robreno in a final letter for appeal. I revealed to Robreno that I was conducting an investigation of my own and pleaded for another chance to clear my name. I told him of Dick Ritter's forbidden testimony, of Acampora's confession, and of Bergstrom's shortcomings. I offered my respect to Robreno as a competent judge and asked for similar respect as an innocent man. My final request was denied.

My self-surrender was designated for December 2, 1999 at Allenwood Federal Prison Camp, located in North Central Pennsylvania, only four hours from my home. Within the adventures of life, I have always found that fear loses its substance at the moment one grapples with it.

Chapter 11

ALLENWOOD, PENNSYLVANIA

I visited Allenwood a week before my self-surrender to prepare for the weighted day to come. A long time past, Allenwood Federal Prison Camp had been reputed a posh minimum-security, white-collar prison, catering to the delicacy of white-collar crimes. Witnessing the prison's full shadow, it appeared to be no more. At first sight, the series of one-story buildings mulled through the frosted windows of my Ford, chilling the car and its passenger more than the actual temperature. Weather stains and other inclinations of age offered yet a darker aspect to its gloomy front. The prison seemed to never have known a youthful era.

The long and broken cemented drive was like a ghostly safari, paving an interference of life within a world of death. The grueling collection of brick and block foundations rested, it appeared, at the bottom of a landfill, fenced in by the blackness of a destitute wilderness that reflected the buildings and their inhabitants below. I watched as the barren trees painfully sunk in the winter's howling wind, cautious of their lost elasticity that comes with age. The season could be only partially responsible for the scarcity of wildlife. The few animals detected appeared tamed, or rather lethargic and perhaps even tired. I imagined that a deer's tracks would appear much deeper there than anywhere else in the world.

Even I felt lethargic as the solitary drive delivered me to the prison's main station. The usual greeting of outdoor freshness offended my senses with an overwhelming thickness, comparable to the smell of a hampered wet towel left abandoned for weeks. An air of stern, deep and unredeemable gloom hung over and pervaded the entire compound.

I entered the administration office with cautious tread, until noticing a harsh contrast to the outside world, through the maintained cleanliness of white walls and bright fluorescent lights. I introduced myself to the unexpected smile behind the counter and began my series of preparatory questions. I was told to bring minimal money, about five hundred dollars in cash, along with my own clothes—gray sweatshirts and gray sweatpants with a comfortable pair of sneakers. I was also approved to bring my doctor-prescribed medication. At this point, I was taking medication for my heart, arthritis, cholesterol, blood pressure, and anxiety disorder.

Leaving the institution, my eyes remained focused on the road before me, failing to absorb the surrounding grimness. The information, the smile, and the main station had temporarily blanketed my fears, allowing me to approach, with feigned normalcy, the days ahead.

A week later, my friend and foreman, Danny Filipone, delivered me to the custody of Allenwood Prison as scheduled. Danny and I arrived in late afternoon, reporting to Intake, or R&D, for my paper work, cell assignment, and classification, including a brief mental and physical evaluation. The smile that had greeted me in the main station became more like a dream in a forgotten past. My formal introduction to Allenwood, instead, came from the vulgar scolding of a sour-featured guard.

With a face doubtful to receive even a mother's love, the guard's two-hundred-forty pounds rested uncomfortably within his five-foot-three-inch frame. His red swollen features were immediately in mine, screaming the f-word repeatedly. "Get that f-ing shit out of here," he said, grabbing my duffel bag with my sweat clothes, money, and medication. Going through the bag, he cursed at my meds before taking them, cursed at my money before pocketing it, cursed at my packed clothes, and cursed at the clothes I was wearing before telling me to f-ing take them off. Once stripped down to my underwear, he cursed at the silently struck Danny to get the f- out of there. I saw the tears well in Danny's eyes as he reluctantly turned to leave.

Perhaps I could have also cried for myself, if not so preoccupied with my stripped dignity. I can never recall anger so deeply seeded and intensely consuming as what I felt that day. I can say, without doubt, that I had never felt such strong contempt for any one being as I did for that guard. Continuing with his diabolic nature and foul mouth, the guard handed me a pair of khaki pants three sizes too large, a maroon shirt that hung far below my fingertips, and two black boots of varying size. I dressed, watching myself closely for an external quiver that would reveal the powerful tremble within. I could not know what the next twenty-one months had in store for me, but I did know that I would not be broken on my first day.

Until completely processed, I suffered silently through this guard's continued abuse for several hours. Fortunately, it would be my last occurrence with that particular vulgarity of a man. I was thankful for my big lunch with Danny, when they escorted me to my cell and it became apparent that I would not be fed again that day.

Allenwood's compound consisted of four identical one-story housing buildings, dormitories they called them, rooming three hundred prisoners in each. Within each building were four cubicles of adjoining cells, in which the prisoners were evenly distributed between cubicles. The cubicles were surrounded by one consecutive hallway, scarcely lit from a semblance of two windows that proved to be only glass blocks. The hall was naturally dark and cold with a pervading smell of urine. Its ends met at a singularly shared bathroom that was void of toilet seats, previously lent out for a game of horseshoes.

The inner core of the building consisted of pure concrete and stone, offering the expected warmth associated with the two. Entrances to the encased cubicles could only be found at either end of the rectangular structure in the form of two double steel doors, barely fitting their designated frames. The massive doors dwelled unrested, causing an unusually sharp, grating sound as they moved upon their hinges. Through their massive weight lay all four cubicles, each with their own series of adjoining cells, and separated by only three-foot isles that sported a series of yellow sirens. The proximity of the prisoners impregnated the air with another odor, the bitter pungency of sweat upon unbathed bodies.

My cubicle was just opposite the bathrooms, marrying the urine and body odor for a scent that singed at the hairs of my nostrils. There was no ventilation to promise relief. My cell was identical to the rest, six feet long and five feet wide, with a bunk bed two feet across from matching dual cabinets that were adjoined by a desk. With such limited space, two cellmates could not walk across the room without physical contact. Each room was confined within three solid walls of concrete and a metal cell door with a wire laced glass plate. There were no windows and no way of telling if it was midnight or noon. With cobwebbed corners and dusty floors, the room was dark and dirty, reflecting the thousands of inhabitants before.

The lack of white-collar delicacy became quickly apparent. Ninety percent of the inmates were strung out and serving time for drug charges, my roommate included. I oriented myself through the only means offered, the freedom to roam the grounds. I faked familiarity when I could, and otherwise resolved to follow the crowd. At ten o'clock that first evening, I took advantage of smoking privileges, leaving my cell for the less stale outdoors. The ten by twenty foot smoking yard was empty and I was so thankful for the seclusion. I fought the moon's stoned shadow of surrounding buildings over the blacktopped pavement with warming thoughts of my family. I hoped, for them, that time would go fast. I hoped Liz wouldn't have trouble sleeping. I hoped my grandchildren, now three of them, wouldn't ask too many questions of Poppy's "long business trip." I hoped Danny wouldn't tell them the harshness he had witnessed. I hoped for many things until noticing a jittery apparition rushing toward me.

At first, I thought perhaps it was a ghost, still unschooled in the subtlety of haunting. Rather, it was a guard. "What's your name?" he asked, speaking in the same manner with which he approached.

"Thomas Pileggi," I answered.

"Thomas Pileggi, eh? You missed count. You missed count."

"What are you talking about?" I asked, hesitant in translating meaning to such a quickly spoken series of words. "I miscounted what?"

"You don't know what count is?" the guard more concluded than asked. I told him that I did not and that it was my first day. He asked if I had gone through A&O. I told him that I had not, nor had it been offered. I never knew what the letters stood for; only that A&O was a staff conducted orientation for new prisoners. Correctly assuming my ignorance, the guard explained count to me, my first explanation of any prison policy.

Count is the process in which, on designated hours each day, all prisoners are confined to their cell, allowing the assigned guards to take an accurate count of each individual, like a rancher herding his cattle. My absence had instilled the preliminary fears of an attempted escape. I apologized for the misunderstanding, excusing it as no fault of my own. The guard told me not to be sorry, yet my penance was two nights in solitary confinement—the "Hole." I quit smoking that evening.

My first night in Allenwood was spent in a prison within a prison. The Hole was like a dungeon, thirty square feet of discolored concrete and steel. Two carpenter's horses supported a stained Styrofoam mattress over a plywood sheet, lacking any comfort of cotton or pillow. Just opposite this bed was the leisure of a personal toilet, still soiled rim to base from the guests before. At the foot of the Hole's steel door, there was a sliding steel access meant for passing food, but duping as an ear to the entire row that welcomed the surrounding screams and violent bangs of my neighbors. The flickering splashes of a dirty yellow light bounced from the single hanging bulb, giving life to the graying ceiling above. I unscrewed it, finding for the first time true Darkness. Attempting fetal-like comfort upon my styrofoam bed, my soul suffocated in the air's hot damp stagnancy, while my body fought the freezing stillness of December. I closed my eyes tightly and prayed for two days sleep.

When returned to my cell, it was now two days without any medication. After the confiscation of my own meds, I had been assured that new ones would be prescribed upon a completed physical. Repeatedly, I told guards of my medical needs. Repeatedly, they denied my requests. I was another number in the count, a nameless face with little significance.

I married myself with the masses, acting with a reserve that contrasted my frank nature. As I followed the prison's herd, I was able to receive all my information primarily from them. After three weeks without medical attention, the consequences were apparent. I lost twenty pounds from a lost appetite and a lost ability to sleep. My anxiety disorder huddled a nervous energy within, encouraging increasing external shakes. The likelihood of dizzy spells was incorporated into my daily routine. I was fifty-four years old, going on a hundred. If I were to survive prison, I feared returning to Liz a shrunken man, aged beyond my years.

Christmas came and went in Allenwood with scarce attention. I cared little for the company and less for my surroundings. Personally, I wished the Lord His birthday tidings, called my family, and went about the gruel of daily routine. Only days had passed when I was called to the visiting room. I discouraged visitors from the start. I wanted them to remember the Tom Pileggi of past, not the aging man so disgracefully isolated from society. I humored Liz, Rosemary, and my brother John on the rare occasion. On this occasion, I had agreed to see my daughter, son-in-law, and Krista.

I entered the visiting room, always amused at their attempted charade. It was a striking room, fresh with bright paint, fluorescent lights, and hospital sterility. Square tables with sturdy chairs lined the room in an orderly fashion. The bathrooms were unsoiled with toilet seats intact. Vending machines charged half as much as in the dormitories across the way. From the perspective of the visiting room, Allenwood looked like a fine place to live.

Krista's soft chime accompanied excitable eyes, as she called out to her Poppy. It had only been a month, but I noticed the little girl had sprouted without me. I embraced her, sculpting into her innocent smile and childlike manner. For a moment, I overlooked my surroundings and we visited as if she were at my home. She told me of her new antics, new friends, and new discoveries, while showing me her most recent drawings. A little artist she was, illustrating carefree cartoon animals with very human traits. Time stood still as I cherished every moment of her company with a new sense of revival. It only lasted two hours, until Krista's parting words returned me to my hellish reality. "Poppy, come home," she said with a tone that seemed to gush out of her heart's deepest well. How I longed to go with her, to watch her and her cousins grow, and to share in their childlike innocence. I said goodbye, holding her within the most profound emotion.

I called Liz that evening as I had done regularly in the past, masking the events of prison with a manufactured optimism. Her voice had a pretty music to it, either enlivening me with its sparkle or soothing me with its continual flow of porcelain delicacy. I tried to remember her scent and pictured basking myself in her smile to relieve the chill of so many lonely days. I told her repeatedly that everything would be fine, hoping to believe it myself.

I only revealed the truth of prison to my sister Rosemary, when I called her daily at the office. Rosemary had begun working with me twelve years ago, after early retirement from a prestigious career at AT&T. With my former secretary Helen retired, Rosemary had become my rock, mastering the fine line between oldest sister and associate. She knew when to cradle my sorrow and combat my self-pity. Her sharp wit and photographic memory made her a necessity around the office. In my absence, she ran the business with my son Jimmy, never missing a trick. Rosemary gave me strength, distracting me with business, while maintaining her maternal tone. I clouded Rosemary from the extremity of my ailing health, although she knew I was not receiving medication. She had my own doctor call the prison on several occasions, reinforcing my medical needs. It was of no success.

One particular day, Rosemary was more inquisitive of my health, concerned over the increasingly apparent vocal strain, reflective of my condition. My voice had been barely affected. If only she could see my fading form and my newly threaded hairs of gray. Feeling the footprints of sleepless nights across my dented brow, I assured her that I would be okay. Half jokingly, I questioned killing myself before the prison did it for me. After hanging up the phone, two guards cuffed me and returned me to the Hole. They had listened to my call and found it less amusing than I.

Two days later, they returned a dying man to his cell. My condition crept through every mode of my being, sluggishly counseling me to my cot from morning to eve. The shakes were getting worse and my dizzy spells were more common than not. I was weak and could barely carry the decreasing weight of my body. At that moment,

I thought the prison would be successful in their method of population control. I was tottering to my fall in this retired and desolate portion of reality. The next day, the guards had no choice but to send me to the infirmary.

Since they had no doctors on staff, a medical assistant conducted my long awaited physical. First, I was diagnosed with diabetes, then with liver disease. I had neither. It was five days until my medication was finally administered in "pill call." Pill call was the herd lining up for their medical feed. I was given two ounces of water to swallow a number of nameless pills. The following morning, the dizziness was gone, but my limbs were frozen. Paralyzed and with swollen body, I was unable to get out of bed. The hollow cry from my cell received a guard's attention. With the assistance of others, I was returned to the infirmary. Concluding that I had received bad medication, I remained, void of prescription, for a week's stay. Slowly, the swelling went down and I regained use of my limbs. I was prescribed new medication.

It appeared that all Allenwood medication was bad medication, all cheaply made in the most generic nature. The variety of meds given me so far differed in appearance from my own. They also differed in their effects, allowing me to function, but never feel well. The new medication was beneficial during the evening, finally restoring my lost ability to sleep. During the day, it increased the dizziness to which I was now growing accustomed. I also learned to ignore the sporadic tingling that led to temporary numbness throughout various areas of my body. I still lacked an appetite and continued losing weight, but in view of the cafeteria food, I was not missing much.

My spirits deteriorated with my health long ago. I continued to call Rosemary for a strength that quickly diminished within my environment. I hated Allenwood.

I hated feeling sick every moment of my day. I hated the reality of prison life. Above all, I hated the predominating convicted drug dealers, the foulmouthed inmates of low moral grade that illustrated little respect for themselves or others. I viewed these men as I viewed Ed Rendell, men willing to sacrifice innocent lives for their own advancement. The majority lacked remorse and formed their own controlling clique throughout the prison, assuming ownership of the weight room, basketball courts, and telephones.

One day in line at the chow hall, my concentration on holding a straight tray through unsteadied hands was broken by vulgarities from one of these contaminated mouths. The mouth belonged to a young six-foot ball of muscle, the buffer of the gang. I had seen his bullying antics on several occasions, although I was never myself the victim. He was profanely complaining, probably about the food, but his volume threatened the smaller inmates around him. I looked up at him, beyond his midnight whiskers and rounded nose, to catch his eye. From several inches below, I told him that if he didn't like it, he should go hang himself from a beam. In retrospect, I believe that my boldness, perhaps even stupidity, was an unconscious outlet of my own death wish. Perhaps, I wanted him to kill me on the spot, but he did not lift a hand or say a word to me. Instead, he reported me to the guards and I got another two days in the Hole.

The Hole was getting easier. I began to perceive it as a mind game, training myself to overcome former fears of claustrophobia. Prison seemed a poorly navigated sailing to an early grave; while the Hole, I imagined, was similar to being buried alive. I had taken pleasure from solitude in the past, loving nothing more than simple peace and quiet. The solitude was present, but the quiet was lost to neighboring clatter and the peace lost to my ever-pacing thoughts. Still, I felt very fortunate. I was not a stranger to my own company. More importantly, I enjoyed that company. I appreciated whom I was and what I had tried to achieve in the past. I favored the values that I had struggled to uphold, and their resulting clarity of conscience. I could not imagine being locked away with only a lingering sin to haunt each moment of reflection. Reflection was the only pasttime in the Hole. After my two days, although still weak and far from healthy, I had a renewed determination, a determination to survive.

I had been meeting with the prison psychiatrist weekly since my arrival. Dr. Karpen was eccentric and impressed with my initial evaluation and IQ test. I met with him for his own pleasure as well as mine. I was not looking for a psychological evaluation, only a compatible conversationalist. For the most part, I found it in Karpen. He simplistically delighted in watching me solve various mathematical problems in my head. Numbers were my livelihood and came naturally to me. I never feared numbers, not even when a dolar sign came before them. Karpen had access to all my files, revealing my wealth, despite my measures to keep it hidden. He displayed the naivete of youth and hinted to a materialistic nature. Karpen was as impressed with my money as he was with my math. Neither meant much to me, but he could not understand why I did not flaunt the two.

I began to grow tired of the lifeless passing days. I wanted something to keep my mind and body busy, something that would prevent both of them from going to waste. During a session with Karpen, I had inquired about options for work around the prison. My fragile physical condition kept me from several of the limited jobs available. Allenwood was a wasteland, encouraging the dissipation of human rubbish. It offered only the necessities of survival and failed at any attempt for personal growth. I cared not to be so easily discarded. Karpen, considering my professional experience, placed me in the drafting shop.

The drafting shop was far from rewarding, but it succeeded in passing the time. The warden had asked me to draft a sewer line, one that never would be implemented. Federal law required every building to be connected by a single line. I would have to extend the sewer line half a mile in each direction. Success seemed unlikely, but I refused to argue. I looked forward to the work, reporting to the drafting shop for several hours, five days a week. I reveled in the use of my mind, since my body continued to fail me.

It had been almost two months since I had first arrived in Allenwood, thirty pounds heavier. The prison's medication proved futile against my deteriorating health. The administration had either refused to believe me or just did not care. The medical staff lacked the skill, equipment and knowledge to make me well. I persevered, establishing the most reliable routine possible. An early morning in the drafting shop, my face became lustrous with perspiration, in spite of an intolerable recurring chill. I rose from my stool with the intent of going to the bathroom. It was the last thing I remembered before collapsing.

When I awoke, I saw nothing but a calm white serenity and the golden face of an angel looking over me. I was in Williamsport Hospital with tubes coming out of my nose and arms. The nurse told me that I had suffered either a stroke or a heart attack. I did not care which one, I was just thankful that I had it. I could feel life plummeting in my veins, despite the bedside image of death taking form as an Allenwood prison guard. I absorbed the Garden of Eden before me: pure white walls, shiny tiled floors, clean cotton upon a firm mattress, a huge window with fruitful rays warming my face, a wooden door, sterile bathrooms, and the heavenly scent of bleach lingering in the air. I felt a tickle in my soul from the soft, feathery touch of the outside world. I could not wait to drink clean water from a glass or taste the merits of the hospital's chef. I had never witnessed such beauty in life than from that hospital bed.

Williamsport nurtured both my body and spirit, offering competent medication from the tenderly skilled hands of nurses. It took them only one week to fix the body that Allenwood had taken two months to destroy. The around-the-clock shadow of an appointed guard finally overcame me and returned me to the dreaded gloom of prison. The following day at pill call, I recognized the familiar no-name pills that had made me so sick in the first place. I began to wonder if anyone survived Allenwood.

Within weeks, my old symptoms had recurred as frequently as before. I maintained, mindlessly going through the motions of daily life, as if in a dream. I continued work at the drafting shop, and divided any spare time between the chapel and the scantily stocked library. I indiscriminately read anything that I could get my hands on. The dictionary, the Bible, autobiography, or classics, it mattered not, as long as I could escape the gloom around me in the printed words of fiction or fact, the printed words of a life outside of my own. I was anxious for anything that would camouflage the numerous remaining months.

The bulk of Allenwood guards were not necessary to particularize. Many were distinguishable from inmates through uniform alone. But there was one good man among the staff, the only one worth mentioning by name. Lieutenant Guise was an Allenwood veteran, and to my knowledge the highest ranking guard in the prison. He worked the five till midnight shift, earning inmate regard from his firm, but fair eye. His prepossessing, cleanly shaven face held a humanely intelligent expression. With noble shoulders, supporting physical brawn, he was the kind of person that easily earned the title of a respectable man.

The Lieutenant was old school, running a tight shift to exemplify the value he placed in the job. Nonetheless, he was accessible to both employees and inmates. His compassion could be detected in casual conversation, as were his street smarts. That was part of his charm. He knew the system and the various elements of human nature confined. The Lieutenant could determine the truth from a lie, through body language alone. He was impartial to the particular man, protecting or punishing on actions, rather than personal judgment.

I watched the Lieutenant often, admiring his finesse and skills. However, I never spoke to him longer than the courteous greeting. After my hospitalization, he took a moment to inquire of my health. The small talk elaborated and one way or another, it was revealed that we shared the same birthday. This impressed the Lieutenant enough to offer me a job in his office, working compatible hours to his own. I was looking for another hobby and from what I knew of the Lieutenant, I liked, so I accepted.

The Lieutenant never specified particular job responsibilities. Sometimes I filed, sometimes I drafted, and sometimes we just sat around, enjoying intelligible conversation. After two weeks of working together, the Lieutenant asked me to put aside what I was doing at the time. He offered me a chair and took a seat on the corner of his desk. "Tom, I know about your case," he said. His behavior and tone seemed most unusual. Not knowing what to make of it, I said nothing. "I know about your case and your trial," he repeated, while searching my face for a bit of recognition.

"Oh, yeah?" I asked. "From my file or do you mean you read it in the paper?" My trial had never been a secret and I did not understand the mystery that he was implying.

"Neither," he answered. Cautiously continuing, he told me that his cousin, a female, had sat on my jury. I verified that it was a small world and asked him to identify which person she was. I still remembered the face of each jury member as if they were members of my own family. He described her and I could recall her quite well. Before the conversation had strayed too far from his goal, he added, "I don't think that you belong here." I confirmed that he meant prison and not just his office.

"Oh, I don't think I belong here either," I said. "But, someone does because here I am."

Erecting himself in virtuous self-assertion, he said, "That is what I wanted to talk to you about." I do not know how the Lieutenant had linked me to his cousin, or how long he had known about it before my employment. But, he proceeded to report to me, what his cousin had reported to him.

The day my verdict had been decided, the South Eastern Pennsylvania Transportation Authority, commonly known as SEPTA, had been concluding negotiations with the likelihood of a strike. I knew that the strike's public announcement had been made later that evening. What I did not know was the affect the pending strike had on my verdict. Apparently, the jury's majority had been in agreement on my innocence, including the mentioned cousin. By majority, the Lieutenant meant every member but one, a New Jersey accountant, whose face I remembered distinctly. His appearance had held all the boredom that his occupation had implied.

According to the source, the New Jersey man had not necessarily been convinced of my guilt, as much as he had been sympathetic to the government. In hopes of a negotiation, he had suggested settling with at least one conviction on the government's behalf. The others of the jury and he had taken turns in bouts of persuasion, to no avail. It was reported that the New Jersey man, in demonstrating his stubbornness, had finally resorted to the threat of transportation. He had told the other jury members that he had a car and could stay to argue the issue all evening. As it was told to me, the jury had compromised my innocence for their convenience, anticipating only a probationary sentence.

I was paralyzed a moment, grasping for the proper emotion, as the Lieutenant completed his tale. I supposed that I was angry, definitely angry, because my freedom had been sacrificed for the sake of public transportation. At the same time, I felt a certain relief. I was relieved to know my innocence had prevailed through the lies. I had never been able to fathom the guilty verdict, since the prosecution had relied on perjury and loose conjecture. The Lieutenant's report, along with his faith in my integrity, offered a valued support that remained with me along the way. I continued working for the Lieutenant, loyal until my time there ended.

In the closing days of March, Dr. Karpen requested an unscheduled office visit. I reluctantly agreed, feeling both physically and mentally fatigued. Karpen seemed more serious than usual, more concerned, and I was thankful that he didn't have mathematical equations on his mind. He told me that Allenwood was not capable of taking care of me properly. I agreed. He said that they did not have the medical facilities necessary. I agreed again, confirming that I expected to die there.

"That's what we're afraid of," he said. "We're looking to ship you out."

"When?" I asked.

"We're working on it."

I left his office barely affected. I learned early on that prison promises hold little value and leaving Allenwood seemed too good to be true. I did not care where they sent me, as long as it was elsewhere. My life depended on it.

Two weeks later, Karpen called me to his office again. When I arrived, he told me that they were shipping me out. I asked when. "Now," he said. I grabbed my few belongings and reported to R&D, this time to prepare for my departure. I concluded that the guards at R&D were the most ignorant, failing to challenge their vocabulary beyond the four-letter word. Through swears, I was again told to strip down and again given prison assigned clothing, the customary orange jumpsuit. The guards cuffed my hands, chained my waist, and both cuffed and chained my feet. They gave me too much credit. I barely had the energy to walk, let alone run. Here stood a sickly, frail old man, convicted of insider trading and chained up like *America's Most Wanted*. The guards enjoyed the image, along with their repeated vulgarity. It made them feel powerful. Before leaving, I responded with two words of my own, attempting to simplify my feelings within the realm of their understanding.

Armed guards escorted me into a barred van, to a small airport and onto a single engine airplane. The hundred and twenty seven pounds left of me was being shipped to the Rochester Federal Medical Center in Minnesota. During my three and a half months in Allenwood, I lost forty pounds; suffered humiliation, a heart attack and paralysis; spent six days in the Hole and fourteen days in medical facilities. Things could not get any worse.

Chapter 12

ROCHESTER, MINNESOTA

R ochester was a Federal Medical Center and prison, much larger than Allenwood with two times the inmates. As a high-security institution, it strengthened its perimeters through reinforced steel gates and a higher staff-to-inmate ratio. Externally, the series of buildings appeared more institutional, with small-aligned windows symmetrically poised across and down several story brick buildings. I did not arrive in Rochester until long after dark and beyond the hours of processing.

The guards led me through a long, well lit underground tunnel that connected all of the institution's seven buildings. The tunnel was fifteen feet high and wide with tiled walls and a concrete floor, reminding me distinctly of New York's Lincoln Tunnel. It directed me to the Hole, where I would spend the night until Administration opened in the morning. Similar in appearance to Allenwood, my sleeping was again confined to a piece of carpenter's hardware and Styrofoam. The long flight had taken its toll on me. It had been thirty-six hours since I had last eaten. The flight's armed guards delighted in coffee and donuts, without conceding to grant me even a glass of water. I was exhausted from the premature March heat and the last remembered fair night's sleep in Williamsport Hospital. The sight of the stained Styrofoam seduced me as comfort to a weary body and mind.

The following morning, I woke to an attractive young woman and a newly faced guard. They took me to Administration for the standard mental, physical, and IQ tests, before escorting me to my cell on the second floor. The second floor looked more like a hospital with its sterile decor and a plenitude of doctors and nurses passing over the polished tiled floors. It housed the medical facility along with several offices, including the Associate Warden's, which meant mandatory air conditioning and with it, ventilation. The air-conditioned chill swept across my face, like a warm fuzzy blanket. I could breathe without the continual suffocation of stagnancy.

My own cell was only fifty feet from the nurse's station, with steel walls and a single steel door that, when closed, protected the room's cold silence. I entered the room and rubbed my eyes to confirm a mirage on the furthermost steel wall. But, there was no mirage. It was a window, welcoming the luxury of natural light. Above it, rested a small louver, not only releasing the stale prison air, but also allowing an inward flow from the fresh outdoors. How cordial the room seemed in comparison to the damp and dark discolored concrete of Allenwood! My spirit felt alive and strong in Rochester, and I had no doubt that my body would soon follow.

The cells were larger at Rochester, twelve by twenty feet, and compensated with an additional cellmate. My cellmates shared the bunks, leaving me the leisure of a singular cot across the room. The two men were similar in appearance and class, convicted drug dealers, sporting matted long hair and beards. One was a bisexual cross-dresser, which bothered me little, until I found him with his pants down, pleasuring himself in the corner of the room. The two often swapped bragging stories of their drug tales, until one day exposed to my opinion.

During one of their swaps, I said, "Knock it the hell off."

"What's your problem, Old Man?" asked the bisexual cross-dresser.

"You are," I said. "I don't like you." I informed them that I was familiar with their type. "I may be old," I said, "but I'm not stupid." I told them they were destroying society's children and the country in general. The conversations ceased, not out of respect for my opinion, but because both of my socially handicapped roommates were soon transferred to other prisons. Their replacements were a young good-natured German boy and an older crybaby lawyer. The lawyer was convicted of overcharging an elderly widow's estate by half a million dollars. I told him early on that it was about time we got one of him in there. The German boy, Carl, seemed to be a good kid. It seemed that things would be looking up. Now, I needed only to concentrate on my health.

I was still, in fact, very sickly. Amidst this huge medical facility, I was unable to acquire any medical attention. I repeatedly attempted appointments with a number of doctors, all too busy to see me. Eighteen days had already passed in Rochester and I was still without medication. My condition seemed apparent to only one woman, Dr. Ruth Westrick. On my nineteenth day, the elderly German woman approached me in the hall, introducing herself as the Associate Warden. She was five-foot-two-inches tall, with an equally minute frame, and she spoke with a foreign gentility unknown to prison walls. She capped her seventy-three years under a fully grayed, tightly wrapped bun. Within moments of conversation, I witnessed the contrast between her age and feisty spirit.

Guardian angels have been known to take rare forms. I believe mine came in this one petite package. Dr. Westrick saved my life with one simple question. "How are you doing Mr. Pileggi?" she asked. I told her that I was not doing so good, that it had been eighteen days without medication, and that it was killing me. "You've got to be kidding me?" she asked. Soon, the entire medical ward witnessed her disguised energy. She grabbed the attention of nurses through loudly spoken orders, all sharing the bottom line, "Get this man taken care of immediately." And, I was.

The medication was properly suited to all my ailments and I began to gain strength, as did my valued friendship with Dr. Westrick. She, like Karpen, was impressed with the results of my IQ test and revealed to me for the first time my 187 IQ. Westrick, most likely a genius, humbled herself to me, through weekly appointments and cherished conversation. Unsatisfied with the limited personal statistics of a prison portfolio, she took it upon herself to research my trial and my past. My experience in landscape design triggered her welcomed suggestion of working in the newly built greenhouse. I agreed, but refused to accept the minimal offer of prison pay. I did not need the money; I needed a hobby.

The greenhouse was close to my cell window. I often delighted in the assorted scents rising from the blossoming flowers below. With my newly restored appetite, I relished the healthy fruits of the soil's labor within the confines of the prison cafeteria. The opportunity to work in the gardens went beyond my anticipations. I looked forward to physical work, especially in the midst of the fertile earth and the vibrant outdoors.

Larry Swenson, an outside contractor on the government's payroll, ran the twelve hundred square foot greenhouse. He was a youthful forty-five years old, with an overwhelming optimism for life that impregnated the cultivation of his garden. Admittedly, Larry was more skilled in the nurturing of flowers and welcomed my expertise in trees and shrubs. There were plenty of both. Petunias, marigolds, lilies, and geraniums massed the greenhouse with color and laced the air with the scent of paradise. Most of the time, Larry and I worked alone, sharing long days and long conversations. We implemented a program, in which we'd travel the tunnel to the "death" building, supplying fresh flowers in the hospital rooms of the dying. They also allowed prisoners to purchase potted plants for their cells. I had three below my windowsill.

Larry and I planted a vegetable and fruit garden that matured into healthy choice entrees in the chow hall. We hired other prisoners to help cart the abundant supply, but when loads disappeared between the greenhouse and the kitchen, we were forced to continue transporting alone. Cucumbers, watermelon, squash, tomatoes, green beans, peppers, radishes and onions were made available to all the inmates, including myself. I felt a springy alacrity working in the greenhouse and it began to show in both my appearance and character. With a refreshed appetite and a nutritious menu, I was again returning to my one hundred and sixty five pounds of ideal weight. I marveled at the life that now surrounded me, such a harsh contrast to the deadly gloom of Allenwood.

I anxiously reported to the greenhouse daily at 9:00 a.m. I reveled in the smell and texture of the soil and refused to wear gloves so I could feel the earth beneath my fingernails. Early one afternoon, I noticed a man approaching as I potted plants. He was an older gentleman, but with the sturdiness of an ox. His seventy-two years were detected only in his long, lean, silver hair, rubber banded into a shoulder length ponytail. Rose tinted tan skin, high cheekbones, and dark rounding eyes emphasized his American Indian heritage, Cherokee, I found out. There was something so familiar about him, yet I knew it was not from Rochester.

My eyes followed him as he observed the surrounding nursery. As he bent over for a detailed examination of nearby plants, the sun threw a shadow over his face. In that moment, I got a preview of the man twenty-five years before. His name was Chief Knight. He owned a trucking business years ago and I remembered him delivering lumber to my sites and shrubbery to my father's nursery. I reintroduced myself and asked what circumstances could bring a successful businessman to prison at such a late age. Apparently, some company drivers had picked up a load in Texas. After stopping in Miami to pick up narcotics, they were arrested in Baltimore. The drivers claimed it was a drug run for the owner. With no other evidence against Chief Knight, prosecutors struck a deal with the drivers. They maintained their freedom and Chief Knight was sentenced to thirty-five years in prison on their testimony.

My perception of Chief Knight as an honest man with sturdy values never changed. We became good friends, sharing frequent walks and the splendor of mature conversation. I enjoyed the education of his culture and religion, when we swapped ancestral tales passed on from our forefathers, comparing similar morals within different contexts. Although stories, tradition, and faith may vary, we shared the value of a common higher power.

After one of his stories, he asked me to keep an eye out in the garden for two eagle's feathers, needed to complete a religious ritual. I agreed, although I had not seen an eagle since I had arrived. He sensed my doubts, assuring me of his prayers that "the big eagle would come." I put in a six-hour greenhouse shift the following day, without a single sight of an eagle. At four-thirty in the afternoon, my roommate Carl entered our cell, interrupting my brief nap after a day's work. He was holding two white feathers, about six inches long and speckled with hints of gray.

"Where'd you get them?" I asked. He told me that an eagle had landed on the tree outside our cell window while he was mowing the lawn. The feathers fell to the ground, and Carl picked them up. I asked why he took them and if he wanted to keep them.

"I don't know why I picked them up," he said. "They looked cool, but I don't know what I'll do with them." After I told him of the Chief's request, he offered to surrender the feathers.

"You're going to take a walk with me to meet the Chief," I said. We found Chief Knight in his cell. Carl's gift was accepted with gratitude but little surprise. I commented on the coincidence and its eeriness, while Carl agreed.

The Chief responded, "I prayed for the big eagle to come." My faith grew a little stronger that day.

Despite my new friendships and increasing hours in the greenhouse, I still found myself fighting the idle passing of time. I was always looking for something more, so I landed another job in laundry, during the early morning hours. Except for cleaning the body bags sent from the death building, I liked laundry. It was a mindless relaxation that offered a certain amusement. Soon after my start, I was proud to receive the title of the fastest shirt folder. Life in Rochester was not so bad. I was treated like a person, rather than a number. The majority of acquaintances made appeared good-hearted, while a few reminded me too much of my days at Allenwood.

One particular guard attempted to test me early on. He entered my cell, and told me to take off my sneakers. When I asked why, he got indignant, informing me that his say so was good enough. In an attempt to avoid trouble, I agreed. I watched as he walked away with my sneakers and threw them in the laundry bin down the hall. Since I still had a pair of slippers and boots, I patiently awaited his next move, checking the bin daily for sneaker status. After seven days, they were still there. A nurse approached during one of my investigations and told me to leave them. Apparently, the guard had gotten hold of my personal statistics and had read up on my financial situation. He was one of those men that hold a personal resentment to anyone wealthier than himself. The nurse told me, that if I retrieved my sneakers, the guard would put me in the Hole. Needless to say, the sneakers stayed.

I started to notice that people actually looked after each other in Rochester and I began to follow the trend. Although only fifty-five, I soon became known as Old Man Pileggi, or just The Old Man. I tried to take care of the younger, less fortunate inmates, buying them candy and necessities that they could not afford.

Tex was one of those less fortunate inmates. He was a tall, lanky fellow and moved with appropriate grace, which made him seem much younger than his thirty years. He never made phone calls, never received mail, and never expected visitors. I felt sorry for him, so I looked after him when I could. I bought him snacks and cigarettes and left my own possessions open for his use. One day, I caught Tex exiting my cell as I entered. After stumbling for a moment, he said that he was looking for me. He wanted to know if I needed anything. I told him that I was fine and he left.

Shortly after, Carl returned to the room and reported someone had stolen my portable radio. I thought it was no big deal. I had already lent the radio and accompanying headphones to Carl on a permanent basis. It was just a radio, easily replaceable. I nonchalantly reported the incident to Tex, more as a warning for his own goods. He became surprisingly excitable, saying, "I'll find him, Tom. I'll find him." I thought perhaps Tex was just anxious for the opportunity to repay me for previous deeds and I told him not to worry about it. Two days later, he returned to my cell saying that the radio was gone. He said that nobody was talking and that he couldn't find any info on it.

"No big deal," I said. "It's just a radio."

"Well, if you don't have the radio, I guess you won't be needing the headphones," he said.

I never told Tex that the headphones were not stolen with my radio, nor were they in his sight. I pulled them out of my locker and gave them to him anyway. When he left, I had another friend down the hall follow him. Tex gave the headphones to a young kid, new to the prison. The kid worked with a buddy of mine at the Chapel, so I had him ask some questions. Sure enough, he had bought the radio with scratched off serial numbers and matching headphones from Tex. I took it as a lesson learned and never pursued the issue. A week later, my new sneakers were stolen.

A guy that worked with me in laundry told me he knew of a pair of sneakers for sale. He answered some basic questions, informing me that the sneakers were stolen Nikes. I concealed my suspicions and told him that I was interested in buying. We set up a meeting for the same evening, in the smoking yard, but he never showed. I laughed at the scenario, as I pictured the laundry guy telling Tex that I wanted to buy my own sneakers back. Tex was a piece of work. Problems with theft were increasing throughout our building and Dr. Westrick looked forward to getting to the bottom of it.

One night, when I returned to my cell, my prison jacket was gone. They found it on a mentally incapacitated inmate. He was wearing my jacket with Tex's lighter in the pocket. Tex ratted the guy out as stealing both. I had no doubt that Tex had set the guy up in an attempt to cover his own tracks, but it was his victim who was placed in the Hole.

I knew what it was like to be punished for something you did not do. The Hole was damaging enough to a man with all his senses. For this man, it could have been fatal. I saw Dr. Westrick in her office and pleaded for the man's release. Refraining from the use of any names, I informed her of the set up and told her that I knew who was responsible. I assured her that I'd get the proof my own way. But until then, I asked that she get the man out of the Hole. She did, putting unexpected faith into my capabilities.

I had my own ideas of how to deal with Tex. I knew his type too well, double dealing and cowardly with a reliance on the naivete of others. Playing his game, I feigned a continued friendship while pursuing conversation with his roommates and associates. I told them that Westrick knew more than she was letting on, that her punishment would be harsh, and that I would not want to be on the other end. Dr. Westrick only knew what I had told her, but I wanted to plant a fear in Tex and anyone else involved.

A week later, one of his roommates came to my cell. He was scared. He knew that Tex had been stealing with three other guys. He feared guilt through association and time in the Hole. I told him that if he talked to Westrick she would probably offer immunity. Better yet, if all three accomplices would join him, perhaps Tex would be the only one held liable. After three out of the four individuals involved sent anonymous letters to Dr. Westrick, offering details to Tex's theft ring, he was sent to the Hole as mastermind. He remained there, for the duration of my stay.

Westrick gave me credit for the savvy of his capture, although I denied any involvement. Dr. Westrick and I continued to meet regularly. She was a remarkable woman with a productive career and a dozen children under her belt. I enjoyed the intellectual conversation, something rare within prison walls. She enjoyed hearing about my business. Before long, she approached me about informally teaching the inmates. It sounded like a challenge and a way to exercise my mind, so I accepted.

Several times a week, she would gather up five to ten interested inmates, most accustomed to only the streets. I took them to a comfortable plot of grass outside and taught them what I knew about math, money, and finance, placing the subjects in a realistic context for their anticipated experiences. I reviewed the basics of buying a home, starting small businesses, and managing money, along with other things. Most of them were receptive students, eager for a new way of life and for a new means of survival in the outside world. Teaching felt good. For my own ego, I felt productive, like perhaps I could make a change. For the students, they had the opportunity to use the minds that prison had laid to waste. I told them about my own humble starts, giving the younger prisoners hope and reminding myself of the fortunes beyond wealth.

On my way to one of these teaching sessions, I prepared to cross paths with a familiar gentleman. When encountering him in the hall several times before, we had exchanged casual greetings. His demeanor seized a remarkable intelligence, poised through the erect posture of a lengthy stature and an accompanying book under arm. Always with books of my own, whether for reading or teaching, I often laughed at the distinctions between us. He appeared to be a similar age, reflecting his professional maturity in a manicured three-piece suit. I, however, lacked the polish of formal education, which I suppose was reflected in my fitted comfort of prison cotton. Yet, both of us seemed to move with a purpose, distracted from the awareness of our immediate surroundings.

Perhaps, it was the teacher's title, or just the confidence it imposed, but I crossed the boundary between us, verbalizing a long curious question. "What are you reading?" I asked after my usual hello, while directing my attention to the constant book under arm.

"*Hope of the Wicked*," he responded, before giving a brief synopsis of the book's political themes. "And you?" he asked. "You seem to have a load of your own," he said, pointing to the number of books I was carting. The majority were business books, used as a tool for teaching, but one was strictly for leisure and shared a similar political base.

"*Drugging America*," I told him and took my turn at summarizing. The book had been given to me from a friend in prison, highlighting inside revelations to the government's corruption in the "war-on-drugs." The author was Rodney Stich, a former member of the Federal Aviation Administration. He had been responsible for air safety at United Airlines on their most senior pilot programs. Since leaving the FAA, Stich had dedicated his life to the investigation and exposure of corruption involving government officials in all three branches of the Federal Government. The book had caught my attention with the mention of Michael R. Stiles, former U.S. Attorney. In 1999, he had announced the unresolved closing of an investigation of four Pennsylvania narcotic agents suspected of criminal activity. Stiles had made no mention of an investigation against the suspected drug traffickers and the evidence accumulated against them. He had erased the entire investigation, with no questions asked and no answers offered.

Seeming fairly impressed at the depth of my reading, the bookish gentleman introduced himself as Dr. Imp, one of the staffed psychiatrists. It was an odd name for a pleasantly odd character, yet to define the name through dictionary alone would be an irony to his very nature.

"We should sit and talk sometime," he said. I feared intentions of a psychiatric analysis, until he added, "informally, of course." In the seclusion of shaded trees, we met regularly for "brain meetings," swapping books and discussing our particular conclusions. *Hope of the Wicked* by Ted Flynn was a curiously extreme political text, dealing with past and present government influences in the establishment of a One-World Order. The book's religious overtones reflected Dr. Imp's own spiritual nature, as an institutionally religious man with a strong code of ethics. My own religion was less bound, found within people and situations, rather than the confinement of a particular building or a structured channel of worship. Our discussions were often intense, sharing, but never imposing, our professed spiritual and political views.

Dr. Imp offered confirmation to my own more reserved thoughts. Our meetings allowed for confidential criticism of the government and their influences on worldly events. Dr. Imp reinforced a similar philosophy to my old friend and jeweler, Tony Fratone. Fratone, as a member of the John Birch Society, believed in the concept of less government and more responsibility. Fratone and Imp discouraged the prevalence of American blind trust, emphasizing personal liability to the nation and its policies. By steering away from the powerfully rich and influential political elite, the national fate would fall in the hands of the dominating lower classes. The success of their theory relied on education and truth, education of social reality and truth of its consequences. Fratone had remained loyal to my education within the thirty years of our friendship. Imp attempted to do the same.

I found certain veracity to the social truths both teachers attempted to employ, yet remained faithful to my own ideals and experiences. I took from Imp what I could and perhaps left him with some new questions of his own. However, we did agree on certain issues: the downsizing of America, the lacking experience in government, the driving force against blue collar and middle class society in the form of unemployment and inflation, the decreasing value of the dollar, and the resulting loss of family values. Above all, we believed that the United States needed to take care of the United States first. Increasingly, we witnessed our tax dollars going overseas, while our own homeland was polluted with social disease, unemployment, crime, increased cost of living, political corruption and materialistic values.

We discussed that society was too quickly judging by class rather than character. Success measured by the dollar increased social ignorance of the quality of life and of personal achievements. In this respect, I conceded to my teachers. A government for the people requires involvement from the people, the masses and not just the wealthy elite. Education and truth is the key to not only a successful government, but also a successful life. Like Plato, I believe that "truth is the beginning of every good thing, both in heaven and on earth and he who would be blessed and happy should be from the first a partaker of the truth, for then he could be trusted."

When the truth is not being upheld in government, whom can we blame other than ourselves, the United States citizens? We are the voters, the financial providers, and the party supporters. If there is ignorance, it is because we fail to seek education. If there is dishonesty, it is because we do not pressure the truth. If there is corruption in the government, it is because we remain timid within the shadow of power. I agreed with Imp in more responsibility, but more responsibility for the government that we created.

My meetings with Imp always concluded with a stronger understanding of myself. It brought back passions forgotten within the cold steel of prison walls. I did not just question the role of government, but my role in life and my abilities to make it better for generations to come. I was not naive enough to try to change the world, merely educate its members— myself included. My teaching echoed my revived understanding, encouraging other inmates to take responsibility for their education, their actions, and ultimately, their selves.

I came to accept my own responsibility in life's circumstances, particularly prison. Although innocent, I found the finger pointing always returned to one man, Tom Pileggi. I had taken on the battle for Cheltenham. I had agreed to work with Rendell. I had responded to his public challenge. I had put my own blind faith in the humanity of man. And, I had hired my incompetent attorney. Although my fate was tainted by influential elements, it was definitely I who was serving the time and it was I who resolved to make the best of it.

By all means, Rochester was prison, illustrating its restrictions daily in mail call, pill call, and count, in the shared restrooms and showers, in the lines for the phone or food, and in the complete absence of any person who truly cares. I was Tom Pileggi, man and inmate, exposed in my barest nature to the prison world. There was no business or family, no expectations or reputations, and no responsibility to anyone but one's self. It was a nakedness of spirit; a vulnerability that led to newly constructed identities, void of social influence. I was no longer the wealthy builder, only Old Man Pileggi known for my immediate merits and displayed character alone. Ironically, the absence of freedom led to personal liberation.

I was beginning to understand the inmate psyche of those who never cared to leave. When confined long enough, the real world becomes make believe, with prison as the isolated reality. Men are released to a society that has lost its logic. They are forced to resume identities that have long been destroyed. I assumed that was Harry's fear.

Harry was a seventy-two-year-old Jewish man that celled across the hall. His only distinction was a pair of dragging feet, ill equipped to support his tottering knees and the weight of his aging legs. Harry was a prison veteran, incarcerated since the early seventies. For what, I never asked. I only knew that he was alone in life, having lost his family to the years. He was a gentle old man, with a tender resemblance to any grandfather. His release was approaching and I thought that he'd do well in the outside world.

The day before his release, Harry came to my cell, asking if I could talk to Dr. Westrick for him. He had nowhere else to go and was looking to extend his stay. I knew that Westrick was vacationing in her mountain home and would not be back for ten days. I certainly did not know how to reach her, nor did I know of anyone who did.

"But I'm getting out tomorrow," Harry said. I apologized, wanting to help, but not knowing what I could do.

"You want to go eat with me, Tommy?" he asked, as he had done several times before, since I too often ate alone. Harry was old enough to be my father, but he held a youthful innocence, a suggestion of a second childhood, that grasped my sympathies.

"Yeah, we'll go eat," I said, walking slowly for his dragging feet to keep up. Harry was a quiet guy. He never talked much, which is why I imagined he took a liking to me. There was comfort in our silence because we never needed to speak for speaking sake. We ate in the pleasure of each other's company. I told him that I would be sorry to see him go, especially since he really wanted to stay. He gave a simple shrug of the shoulders and asked if I wanted his dessert. Although moved by the gesture, I declined, telling him to eat it himself.

After dinner, we returned to our cells at 7:30 p.m. I remember because I had looked at my watch just before calling Rosemary from the phone booth down the hall. Only moments into my call, I caught Harry waving hello to me as he walked past. I laughed and waved back. What a funny little guy, I thought. I had no doubt he'd do fine upon his release.

Ten minutes later, my conversation was interrupted with a bang on the side of the booth. It was one of the smaller guards. "You got to help me, Pileggi," he said. "You got to help me. Suicide! Suicide!" I dropped the phone and followed him to the janitorial closet, the slop closet as we called it. It stored all the mops, buckets and brooms and was supposed to be locked at all times, but was not then. The guard continued to jerk at the door that repeatedly budged only inches before snapping shut. From the guard's comments and the door's tension, I knew the weight of death lay on the other side. I stopped the guard from his thoughtless yanking. With every pull of the door, he was elevating the body and tightening the noose. If the suicide had not succeeded the first time, this guard was ensuring its success time and time again. I told him that we had to take the door off the hinges and sent him for the tools. He returned only moments later. We unfastened the door, untied the attached sheet, and watched the lifeless body hit the floor. It was Harry.

Harry had not been waving hello, but goodbye. His offer of dessert was a final motion of friendship, one that I had declined. Poor Harry had set up the whole thing before our discussion. After sharing his last meal with me, he had set off to a waiting sheet in an unlocked closet, finding the only life suited him after so many years in prison. Harry was buried at Rochester without a service.

The only visible consequence of his death was an increase in guards and an increase in restrictions. The prison attempted to avoid the contagiousness of suicide. The attempt was not necessary. Most of us knew that, in regard to prison, Rochester was a fine place to live. I thought a lot about Harry, about the man that few, if any of us, ever got to know. Prison envelops you in a continual stream of fellow men, whether inmates, guards or staff; yet, it is the loneliest place for one to live. It is isolation beyond the interaction of man, isolation within the deepest crevices of the mind and heart. I have yet to witness a more tragic jailor than one's self.

I had already been in Rochester for five months; eight and a half months in the Bureau of Federal Prisons, yet, I felt as if it was a lifetime. I was not even half way through my sentence, when I was summoned to a case manager's office to receive a conference call from my sister, Rosemary. She was calling on behalf of an attorney, who claimed to know the prosecutor in my case and could negotiate my freedom in exchange for a settle-. ment with the Securities & Exchange Committee. If I paid triple their estimated damages, my assumed profit with interest, I could go home. He assured me that the six hundred thousand dollars would in no way be an admission of my guilt. However, it did not seem like a denial of it either.

Before the trial, I could have settled for only twenty-five thousand dollars more and avoided the civil case. I refused that deal for the same reason as this one; both implied a financial retribution for a crime that I did not commit. Money was not the object; my innocence was. I'd be lying to say the offer did not tempt me. I was tempted to the point that I asked the lawyer to put my freedom in writing. He refused, as did I. I had no interest in compromising my integrity at the passing of a buck.

Two days later, Rosemary and my brother John flew up for a visit, figuring that they would have a better chance in person. They argued my refusal to the lawyer's offer and begged me to reconsider. For them, my issues of integrity were not worth the time away. They pressured me with their own arguments and included the lure of my wife, my grandchildren, and my business. "For my family," as they put it, I agreed to discuss the offer with the lawyer one more time.

Again, his proposal was received through Rosemary's conference call, bargaining my freedom for a financial settlement. The money was not required for forty-five days, but my signature was required immediately. The signature insured my commitment to pay, along with my silence. Essentially, I was signing a gag order, forbidding me to disclose any elements of my case, conviction, or settlement. With my family's united voice still lingering, I reluctantly agreed. The lawyer made all the arrangements and sent the appropriate documents, none of which mentioned my guaranteed release from prison. I was forced to rely on his word alone. Under supervision, I signed each document, feeling my face darken in the light of a new prison.

Thirty days later, I was still in Rochester, when I was summoned again for my first direct call from the lawyer. He told me that my release would rely on one last detail, a testimony against Fred Dreher for perjury. I had to testify that Dreher had lied at my trial when claiming I was not present at the November 1 meeting. "We'll get Dreher for perjury and you'll go free," he said.

If I were to be placed into a movie, it would be as victim of a horror. The entire audience would warn me not to open the door, yet I would, to face the disfigurement of a machete-holding murderous fiend. In retrospect, I see the continuing pattern of my mistakes, the continuing pattern of misplaced trust. I gave them their promise and money, and now they wanted me to commit perjury as a means to implicate Dreher on false charges, at the same time implicating myself. My relationship with Dreher was limited to Cheltenham, but within those limits I found only a decent human being. From what I came to understand, Dreher's downfall had been his Philadelphia success in raising funds for the Republican Party. I was beginning to fully understand the way men like the lawyers and prosecutors operated. With cautiously chosen words, I told the lawyer what he could do with his offer. "I'm not a Greenwood," I told him, and would not take part in his body for a body philosophy.

I researched my options in suing Poluka for prosecutor misconduct. In addition to his bogus deal, in my opinion, he willingly allowed Greenwood and Larsen to commit perjury on the stand. In my opinion, Poluka and his ethics were one big obstruction of justice. In my research, I found that since the assistant district attorney acts on behalf of the district attorney, any liability was seen as a detriment to others in the field and would prevent them from performing their functions. Since 1952, it had been held that high public officials, prosecutors included, are immune from suits seeking damages for actions taken in the course of their official duties. Poluka was untouchable. He could break the law without consequence and find protection from legally mandated immunity.

Fifteen days after my last conversation with the attorney, Rosemary was required to sign the check as my power of attorney. The papers were signed, and although my freedom would not be granted, my financial obligations still stood. Instructed by me, Rosemary wrote, "PAID UNDER PROTEST," across the bottom in bold, capital letters. They cashed the check anyway, and I gladly remained in Rochester, for the time being.

Shortly after, I met Dr. Westrick in her office. She told me that she wanted to move me closer to home, somewhere my family could visit more often.

"I won't go back to Allenwood," I told her.

"Of course not, Tom," she said. "But, Virginia would be the next closest place."

I had heard a rumor that any prisoner leaving Rochester was first taken to Kansas City, where they remained in the Hole, waiting transfer to a series of other prisons. With each prison came more time in the Hole, until reaching the final destination. I asked Westrick to confirm the degree of truth to the rumor.

She dismissed it with a chuckle and said, "Tom, you've done a lot of good around here. The only thing I've ever seen you guilty of is good deeds. I'm going to give you a furlough," she said, "so you can leave on your own." The furlough meant that I could transfer myself to the new prison, unguarded. I would be released on my own recognizance, reporting at a designated time to Petersburg Federal Prison Camp in Virginia. Three days later and six and a half months since arriving at Rochester, I reported to R&D for a 5:30 a.m. transfer. Westrick arrived soon after, making sure that I had the proper medication and filling me in on what to expect. She offered me a ride to the airport, but a taxi was on its way. Before she left, she shook my hand and said goodbye.

I changed into civilian clothes and waited for the arrival of my cab. The taxi was taking me to Minneapolis airport. After an hour and a half layover in Detroit, I would fly to Petersburg. I was free, not even for a full day, but still free. In my own clothes, with neither guards nor cuffs, I enjoyed the ride through clear sunrise, watching all the sights missed in the past several months. It was a glorious sight—the outside world in a wondrous flourish of people, traffic, open spaces, and all the life that I had been missing. For a moment, I felt that I had never left it. I opened the window and filled my senses with the city's luster, tasting the moist dew drawn air and inhaling the sweet nectar of exhaust. I had never felt so alive and had only Westrick to thank for this brief touch of reality. I was going to miss her and I was going to miss Rochester Federal Medical Center.

Chapter 13

PETERSBURG, VIRGINIA

arrived at Petersburg in the late afternoon, greeted by a gold-toothed Panamanian named Jarvis. He was an inmate and trustee from the prison, sent to ensure my safe arrival to the camp. I convinced him to let me buy him lunch at Burger King, so that I could spend my remaining money before it was confiscated at the camp. We each got Double Cheeseburger value meals. Jarvis had been imprisoned for the past twelve years, and Burger King seemed to be the biggest thrill of his life. The furlough had been mine. I bought six packs of cigarettes, resuming my deadly habit after close to nine months, and gave my remaining ten dollars to Jarvis. He sent it to his daughter with a brief letter. Jarvis seemed like a decent man, probably convicted for a foolish mistake in youth.

As I approached the prison camp, I noticed its resemblance to a colony. Several drives extended to a chain of sporadically situated time-eaten buildings. The maximum-security facility across the way was distinct in its bleak walls and eye-like windows, along with increased surveillance and reinforced double barbed fences. To the left, a sister building was in the process of shabby construction. Different mixes of concrete left the building a smorgasbord of colorless shades of gloom. Soon, weather stained shadows would blend it with the rest of the aging colony.

Jarvis surrendered me to intake, but returned shortly after with a camera, asking the guard to take our picture. Weighing an ideal hundred and sixty five pounds and full of energy, I forgot my surroundings and gave the camera a smile, amusing Jarvis with memories of our brief excursion. Jarvis had been a good introduction to Petersburg, better than the iron curbs of the rest. R&D processing was becoming a familiar procedure. I checked my medication, emptied my pockets, took my tests, waited for room assignment, and accepted my oversized green wardrobe and standard black boots.

The guards whispered a brief conversation before telling me no rooms were available in the overcrowded building. I laughed at first, picturing a no vacancy sign being lit at the prison's entrance. Then, a shiver crept over me, as I wondered if this meant more time in the Hole. Instead, they placed me in a bunk on "the beach." The beach resembled the bottom floor of a several story mall. It was the open lobby, located in the center of the building. From there, I could look straight up, past the five surrounding floors, to a dingy skylight overhead. Generally, time on the beach was used as a punishment. At the time, I was the only one settled there and I liked it. I had no cell to call my own, only a bed, a locker, and a lot of space. From the comfort of my bunk, I could see each floor above and every cell surrounding. It felt safe, without the claustrophobia of a cold steel confinement.

On my second day at Petersburg, I was told that I had a visitor waiting. I had not anticipated anyone, nor did the prison staff. I arrived at the visiting room, finding Joan equipped with an armload of her custom jewelry. She had violated prison policy by giving it away freely to the guards and families of other inmates. Rather than implementing the proper channels, she called the warden directly and insisted upon seeing me. Her visit was appreciated, but not her means of achieving it or the uproar it created.

Joan and I visited for five hours, swapping stories of business and family, before I returned to the beach for interrogation by both prisoners and guards. How did I know Joan? What was our relationship? Would she be returning? It was none of their business, so I chose silence in answer to their rumoring questions. Shying away from the spotlight, I denied Joan's requests for future visits. Instead, I appreciated the storm of supportive letters and postcards sent weekly. She meant well, but prison and celebrities did not mix. I wanted to finish my time as Old Man Pileggi, the unassuming and average inmate.

I was eager to get established in Petersburg, to familiarize myself with the new surroundings and to create an accommodating routine. Part of that routine was the standard daily pill call. Shortly after leaving Joan, I responded to a summons for medication, lining up with the rest of the sickly herd. The guard issued me a handful of pills, none with even a slight resemblance to Westrick's prescription. I told him there must have been a mistake. Dr. Westrick was sure to administer and send the proper medication with me. The guard barely considered my argument, telling me I was in Petersburg and would take Petersburg medication. Without much choice, I conceded, feeling the consequences within days.

Petersburg medical was worse than Allenwood. The pharmacy was located in the high security facility across the way and often they sent the wrong pills in the wrong bottles. Repeated discrepancies in pill color, shape, and size went undetected until forced to the guard's attention, keeping me on constant alert for the wrong medication.

The right medication was detrimental enough. My arthritis was acting up with back and leg pains. I felt nauseous and dizzy, and tended to stumble around with a lack balance. Fearing a medical repeat of Allenwood, I called Rosemary, asking her to get in touch with Dr. Westrick. I did not doubt Westrick's power as an influential woman, but the degree was illustrated when I received the closest generic versions of her previous prescriptions within weeks. I believe she raised hell on my behalf and someone got scared, scared enough to make sure I was taken care of. The generic pills worked well enough that my campaign for medication could be put to rest. My health was restored just in time, as Petersburg became an increasing handful.

For the first few weeks, I watched as close to sixty prisoners were added to the beach, and escorted off, depending on their punishment. Some were added for the same reason as I, relocating with the availability of room. When I was finally offered a cell, I declined, telling them to give it to the next guy in line. I was the only constant among many variables. The beach suited me fine, and I was content to remain there.

At the start of my fourth week, the camp's head administrator, Mr. Weaver, approached me with an offer to teach. Westrick had told him of my success at Rochester, but Weaver was more interested in the formality of a classroom setting. I agreed to teach fifty students three afternoons a week for five-week semesters. Despite my own refusal to accept pay, the prison's budget would not allow for many necessities. I had Rosemary send postal money orders to my prison account, so that I could purchase notebooks and pens for each student. I taught them everything I knew about life; everything learned within my fifty-six years. I focused on staying out of trouble when released, on starting fresh and abandoning the old. I told them how to get a job and how to keep a job, how to start and run a successful business, how to buy a new home and refinance it for a profit, and how to budget and manage the money they made.

I loved teaching, especially since the majority of students were eager to learn. One of my best students was Moses, a sixty-year-old man that I had known from long ago. Over twenty-five years before, Moses had been a chef at a restaurant in one of my developments. I marveled at how small the world really was when I had first seen him in chow hall after so many years had passed. "Is that you, Moses?" I asked. Physically, the years treated him kindly and remained faithful to his firm physique. He had a lingering adolescent smile that spread across his smooth black skin, making him look younger than he really was. For myself, Petersburg had beefed me up with their traditional southern fried food. My cholesterol medication had been thinning my hereditary thick hair at the temples, while the rest began to filter in shades of gray. Moses looked past the transformation and recognized me immediately.

With pronounced African American features, anxious hair, and large liquid eyes, Moses reminded me of Buckwheat from The Little Rascals. I photocopied a picture of him found in the library and tacked it to Moses' cell wall with the inscription, "Moses! The real Buckwheat." Soon, he was responding regularly to the nickname and I, in turn, was given the name, Spanky. As Spanky and Buckwheat, we were inseparable, sharing meals, knowledge, and the events that had brought us there.

Moses had fallen in love with a woman hooked on drugs. He had tried to get her clean for the sake of her two children and, for a time, had thought that he succeeded. As a respected chef, he worked the unorthodox hours required of a restaurateur, while increasing financial assistance to his girlfriend and her offspring. Often, Moses stayed with the woman in a home shared by her brother. Unknown to Moses, the brother had a similar addiction that he supported by dealing drugs from out of the house. All of them were caught in a police raid. Moses was in the wrong place at the wrong time, which resulted in a six-year prison sentence. The woman went free.

Moses held no resentments and continued to send her the little money available to him within the confines of prison community. He remained faithful to her, while it was my understanding that she remained faithful to drugs. I repeatedly taught in my classes that the key to staying out of trouble was staying away from the characters that led to trouble. Moses' girlfriend was one of those characters. I convinced him to break all ties with her and, through written correspondence, introduced Moses to the cousin of another inmate. The cousin was a respectable sixty-two year old widow, working with the NAACP. They wrote frequently before she drove down for a visit. It was love at first sight. Today, the two plan a wedding upon his release.

Although Moses found love, his ordeal was as trying as my own, particularly since we were both advancing in age. Despite his trials, Moses remained faithful to Allah as the "best of planners."

"It is His work," Moses said, "which brought you here to share with us the many blessings that He has given you." Moses gave me credit for the education I supplied, unaware of the education which I received. Convicted on circumstance, rather than deeds, he had remained faithful to his God, the people that surrounded him, and ultimately, to himself. Moses was only one of many inmates that illustrated this strength in the face of a raw deal.

Earl Whiddet was seventy-two years old and a lawyer; Martin Luther King's lawyer in his youth. He had been sentenced to thirty-seven months on ninety counts of mail fraud and lost his license to practice law. Whiddet had been hired as an escrow agent for a company in California. The company had been selling and, apparently, shipping exercise equipment to Virginia, but the goods never reached their destination. When Whiddet found out the company was bad, he refunded each of the ninety deposits. As a lawyer, his honesty had been viewed as illegal. His guilt had been founded on one count of mail fraud for each returned deposit. Whiddet had arrived at Petersburg three weeks after me, financially wiped out by the destruction of a life long career.

Waiting on word of an appeal, he told me that he was taking one day at a time.

"God has been good to me," he said, "and I do feel blessed." I used to hide some prison luxuries under his pillow, bags of chips, cans of tuna, bars of soap, and anything else he could not afford. After finding them, he would come to me and say, "Tom, you didn't have to do that."

"Do what?" I would ask, denying any involvement. I was not after the credit. I viewed it as helping an unfortunate old man, who remained optimistic beyond his circumstances.

Bernard, or Born as he came to be called, was another unfortunate soul, finding hard luck since his youth. His father was a New Jersey State Trooper, and his mother was a homeless drug addict wandering the streets in prostitution to support her habit. Born lived a normal life with his father until his teens, when he left to find his mother. His intentions of rehabilitating his mother backfired with his own introduction into the drug underworld. He was soon addicted, selling drugs on the street to support his maternal heritage of drug dependence.

At twenty-one years old, Born had been sentenced to eight years in prison for conspiracy to sell drugs. He was twenty-seven when I met him, with the body of a prized fighter and a countenance not easily forgotten. His handsomeness matched his intellect, both matured decades beyond his lived days. With only two years left in prison, he told me, "I am determined to rise above my condition, even though the odds are against me."

This determination was witnessed his first day entering my class, when he said, "My only request is that you provide me with information that will be beneficial to my growth and development. I desire to be informed," he said, "so any material that you know will be educational, please give to me." I did my best, not only for Born, but for all of them. I hoped that the students, the majority of them, would leave each evening with a hope for more, an attainable more outside of the world of crime and drugs.

Since the classroom focused on a general education, adapted to suit the interests of many, I set up tutorial sessions for both inmates and staff with specific needs, particularly in starting their own businesses. We would gather informally on the lawn and swap ideas and suggestions. As a sign of respect, the students called me Mr. Tom. The name stuck, as I became increasingly well known to the prisoners and guards. Generally, I was liked by most, except for Mr. James.

Mr. James was one of the guards and my hugest nemesis. Only ten years younger than me, he stood six and a half feet high with an ego equal to his size. Full of piss and vinegar, he could be described only as pure bully with weasel eyes. Reading my personal stats, he knew early on of my financial wealth. Consequently, he had it out for me from the start and my growing popularity made matters worse. James was the hump on my back and the thorn in my side. We loved to hate each other and offered the appropriate sentiment found within lifelong foes.

James instilled me with an annoying amusement rather than fear. I was always up for his match of wits and the opportunity to humble him in front of other inmates. Our first confrontation was during an outdoor tutorial, where sixteen of us sat on a plot of grass behind the commissary. Ignoring my fellow inmates, James approached me with a poorly hidden grimace that accompanied his words. "Pileggi, off the grass" he said. I asked why, since it was not a violation of prison policy. "Because I said so," he answered. I tried to explain that I was tutoring.

"I don't care what you're doing. I want your white ass off the grass," he said.

"What about everyone else on the grass?" I asked, looking around at the inmate-strewn lawn.

"I don't care about them, Pileggi," he said. "Just you, and if you don't, you're going to the Hole."

Instilled with the courage that only crowds give, I said, "You're a trouble maker. You know that, James? I'm not afraid of you." His small ferret eyes danced with delight as he pulled out his cuffs and constricted my hands in front of me. I could feel the extra bounce in his step, keeping my rhythm in tune, as he led me across the street to the maximum-security building. He checked me in with the appropriate guard to secure my placement in the Hole. On route, we passed the open office door of Mrs. Robero, the Associate Warden. All administration and staff were addressed with conventional titles before their surnames, reinforcing the strict barriers of formality. Mrs. Robero and I briefly caught eyes before she called my name, saying that she wanted to speak with me. The guard accommodated her request, placing me before her.

"Mr. Pileggi," she said. "I just wanted to tell you that we appreciate all the teaching you are doing over there." Looking first at the guard and then at my constricted hands, she asked, "What are you doing over here?" I told her that I was being escorted to the Hole and explained the circumstances behind it. I also apologized that I would not be able to teach later that afternoon.

"Don't be ridiculous," she said. "You're not going to the Hole." She instructed the guard to return me to camp and requested Mr. James in her office. As the guard escorted me out, she said, "Let me know if you ever need anything, Mr. Pileggi."

I returned to the camp and the same plot of grass where my students and Mr. James remained. "You're supposed to be in the Hole," James said. I told him that I was preparing to teach and that I would appreciate him getting off my back.

"Furthermore," I added, "Mrs. Robero would like to see you in her office." James looked at my accompanying guard for a nod of confirmation, as the corners of his mouth aridly drew down. "You don't like me James, and now I don't like you," I said. His face reddened with his rising temper before leaving to answer his summons. Profanities were heard flying all the way. I returned to my students, knowing it would not be my last confrontation with Mr. James.

Mr. James followed me everywhere, looking for any opportunity to get me in the Hole. I was the model inmate and cautiously observed prison etiquette, frustrating James all the more. He grasped at any straw that I offered. One morning, about 3:30 a.m., the unstoppable ring of the guard's platform phone woke me from a restless night's sleep. A young female guard, about my daughter's age, was on duty that night. I mechanically rose and sleepily wondered why she failed to answer the phone. A female guard in a male prison worried me for the obvious reasons. Since she was nowhere in sight, I answered the phone, still half asleep. The persistent caller had hung up, either at the sound of my voice or just before. I walked the circumference of the beach, investigating the area and the security of the locked doors, but still no guard.

Twenty minutes later, I was waiting at the platform, figuring my next move, when she came out of the bathroom. Her face was pale and her person disheveled, giving the impression that she had been sick. I asked if she was okay and told her that I had picked up the ringing phone. She had heard it ring as well, but her condition left her unable to answer. "Are you sure you're okay?" I asked. She assured me that she was and thanked me for my concern. I returned to my bunk without giving the incident a second thought.

At noon, on that same day, Mr. James came to the beach looking for me. "Pileggi," he yelled. "Did you pick up this phone last night?"

"What are you talking about?" I asked. "I didn't pick up any phone last night."

"Any prisoner picking up an unauthorized phone goes to the Hole," he said.

"Well, I didn't pick up that phone last night," I said. He told me that he knew I did, which I had no doubt. "I didn't pick up the phone last night," I repeated. "I picked it up at three thirty this morning."

"Oh, you want to be a smart ass?" he asked, as his face altered with anger. I told him, "No," and distinctly explained the difference between morning and evening using midnight as the signifying divider. He started flaunting his vocal chords, letting all the surrounding cells hear of his intentions to put me in the Hole. I, of course, argued that I was merely trying to help the girl. But, he did not want to hear it and, to his own disadvantage, made his entire argument boisterously heard. Mr. Weaver and my case manager, Mr. Tucker, heard the yelling from their offices and came out to investigate. They had been informed of the phone incident earlier that morning from the female guard leaving duty. They were also aware of James' dramatic displays against me. Tucker interrupted James' antics, telling him that I was just concerned about a guard and to leave me alone. Tucker's words were the last and James again stormed off. The score was Pileggi two and James zero.

Mr. Weaver called me to his office after the James incident and asked if I cared for a job in the warehouse. Teaching and tutoring were rewarding, but still only a part time job. I needed something else, something to fight the slow moving hand of Father Time. The warehouse seemed to be the best of my choices. Among the other choices was UNICOR, the most popular occupation at Petersburg, and one that I cared little for. It was a self-sustained prison factory manufacturing anything from textiles to office furniture. The prison prided itself on employing and providing skills training to the majority of inmates, while keeping them constructively occupied. The hours and labor were similar to any factory job, but the pay was not. At UNICOR, inmates made only cents an hour, producing quality goods for sale to the Federal Government. I would not have accepted the pay, nor have minded the work, but I had something against the principle of legalized slave labor. A day's work barely paid enough to purchase a bar of soap. I watched inmates return to their cells, after exhausted from a grueling day's work. In reality, they swapped their hard labor for the minimal necessities of life, and would leave prison as destitute as they entered. I wanted no parts of it, and accepted the warehouse job with enthusiasm.

The warehouse had a history of inventory problems, despite being run primarily by prison guards. When offering the job, Weaver asked me to focus on inventory control. Initially, the task seemed like an easy one, since they only conducted inventory once a month. I began a daily record of everything imported to and exported from the warehouse. I asked the prison paid officers to weigh each item they were bringing in off the trucks. They refused, claiming it was too time consuming and unnecessary.

Time was irrelevant to me. Since I had plenty of it, I weighed the items myself, accounting for everything delivered. I noticed flour was repeatedly arriving up to three thousand pounds short of the order. Banana crates were prematurely opened with six to seven bananas missing at a time. The officers delivering the items and the officers accepting had a great rapport. They were content with their monthly inventories and recurring short trucks, and I realized why my suggestions were never welcomed. The inventory problem was not with inmate theft as Weaver had supposed. Items were disappearing before they ever made it into the warehouse.

I designed a computerized bar code method of tracking incoming and outgoing products and approached Weaver with the idea. Computers were not in the prison's budget; nothing was, so I volunteered the equipment from my own funds. It was denied as a violation of prison policy. I settled for a card program, logging master inventory on yellow index cards that I bought myself. I was the only one to follow the program, as tension increased from the warehouse guards. "Mr. Tom" became "Pileggi" and the thin patience to my ideas was more commonly verbalized. An inmate finding punishable lodging on the beach told me that I was the fifth guy in the past year to fill that position. The last four started with the same good intentions and all ended up in the Hole. It was a path that I did not care to follow.

I saw Weaver after only two weeks and asked if I could quit. I told him that I was not pointing any fingers, but there was a racket going on and I wanted out. He understood well enough and accepted my resignation. I was again left with idle time and asked if there were any other positions, other than in UNICOR, for which I was qualified. He offered a position in the powerhouse for twelve cents an hour. "Keep the money," I said, "but I'll take the job."

The powerhouse was built like the Rock of Gibraltar, with concrete floors and thick block walls. My job consisted of sporadic meter readings and water level checks on the boilers that dominated the internal structure. Most of the time, I would be alone, sitting at a desk. I welcomed the solitude and the rare silence that allowed me to busy my soul in dreams—reading and writing. I worked the night shift five days a week and inmates soon planned their showers around my schedule, knowing it was the only time they were guaranteed hot water.

My schedule offered another guarantee to a friend that I named Chico. Chico was a docile mouse with the Latin features of a tan complexion and dark eyes. I first met him while eating a cheese sandwich and ginger snaps between chapters of my current read. His proximity startled me as he sniffed around my desktop in search of leftover crumbs. I offered him a slice of cheese that he refused. He knew a sucker when he saw one and held out for a ginger snap. I crumbled up the cookie and watched as he ate silently. From that day on, I kept a box of ginger snaps in the desk drawer, guaranteeing his treat with each recurring visit. We shared many late nights of silent company in the powerhouse, two solemn fellows fighting the infection of prison's ghastly hue.

After a particularly late night with Chico, I took advantage of the night shift perk and slept in. I was stirred into semi consciousness after hearing the voices of Mr. James and Big Ed, the prisoner bunking to the left of me. Big Ed was asking James what he was doing with my shoes and clothes, reminding him that my work schedule allowed me to sleep later. Just before dozing off again, I heard James silent Big Ed's argument as he cautiously wrestled with a plastic bag. I woke again, at about 9:30 a.m., and saw Big Ed sitting on the edge of his cot. He was waiting for me to wake up and I wondered if he had watched me the entire hour since James left.

"Mr. James took all your clothes," he said. "I tried to stop him. I told him it wasn't right, but he just told me to be quiet." I told Big Ed that I had heard them talking an hour before. "Why didn't you stop him if you were awake?" he asked.

"I wasn't up for the argument," I told him. "Don't worry about it, Ed. Mr. James is what he is." However, in the meantime, James had left me barefoot and without a prison assigned uniform. I decided to speak to Mrs. Pollen, a camp administrator that I had run into several times before.

When I showed up at her office, the first things she asked was what was wrong and why wasn't I wearing any shoes. "I'm lucky to be wearing what I have on," I told her. "Mr. James wiped everything out." She asked why, agreeing that prison policy allowed me to sleep in when working night shift.

"I'll take care of him," she said and I returned to my cot. Shortly after James returned with my stuff.

"You're a piece of work," I told him, "I don't know what I'm going to do with you." He told me that one more word would get me put in the Hole. "At least I'd have peace and quiet without you bothering me all the time," I said. James conceded to his normal huff and scuff, while complaining that he could never have any fun. That was James's idea of fun, picking on inmates and those weaker in the system. James had created a prison for himself, one in which he was neither respected nor esteemed, but rather the tragic victim of his own personality. Most guards were considered underpaid, under appreciated, and under trained, but James got only what he deserved.

I wondered if it was Mr. James having fun again when my bunk area was ransacked a month later. Returning from the powerhouse, I found my teaching lessons scattered across my bunk with other papers. My chair was missing and my locker turned upside down, spilling its remaining contents across the floor. Johnny Blades was a convicted drug dealer, who slept only two bunks down from me. He was about twenty-eight years old and liked by few. Everyone called him Nine Lives because he always managed to find his way out of trouble. I felt sorry for the kid and left my locker open, so he could help himself to candy bars.

Johnny had seen everything and made a point of telling me so. When I asked who was responsible, he said that he would not rat. "I'm not asking you to rat anyone out," I told him. "I just want to know where my stuff is." My locker was left unlocked for him in the first place, giving the perpetrator full access to my goods. If James was responsible, his nameless act earned no credit for courage. Johnny remained stubborn and I took my own advice, staying away from troublesome characters.

Friends were not an issue. I had made good ones in Petersburg, the best since my incarcerated journey.

Moses, Born, and I had become the New Rat Pack, carousing the prison together like boyhood pals. We all shared an appetite for knowledge and good food. However, good food was not to be found in chow hall, only outdated scraps that could be batter dipped and fried. We compensated, satisfying our hunger in education with frequent trips to the library. After noticing new blacktop being laid in the parking lot behind the medical building, I sent Moses and Born ahead one day. The medical building was three stories high, but the rear rested at ground level. Like the rest of the buildings, it was surrounded with age worn concrete walkways, disturbed with cracks and crevices.

Only weeks ago, I fixed a similarly fractured walkway, outside of the visitor's building, that had a crevice five inches wide and deep. I found my way into maintenance and borrowed the necessary materials, mixing my own version of concrete from cement and sand. Gaining some attention, but little trouble, I mended the long neglected path. Petersburg's entire foundation ached for cosmetic reconstruction, but with limited time and material, I had settled to fix only the most hazardous.

The men that I watched behind the Medical Center were laying their blacktop higher than the weather tattered cement. The parking lot sloped downward and the new drains were placed at its peak. I told the men that the first rain would descend with the earth's curve and flood half the medical building. They were contractors hired outside of the prison community and they illustrated the closed minds of outsiders. "We don't talk to prisoners," the one man said.

"Well you might want to talk to me, because you're not doing the job right," I told him.

"What do you know?" he asked and continued his work without waiting for my response. I told him that I knew a lot, but none of the men seemed to care. They finished their job, displaying the same ignorance with which they had started. I went to see Mr. Weaver to explain the situation. I warned him that the blacktop was too high and the drains misplaced. Weaver may have doubted me, but he pretended to understand the severity of a potential flood. Nonetheless, he inquired what could be done to prevent it. After I offered my solution, Weaver said that he would talk to maintenance.

He did not get back to me until a week later, after the first heavy rain. The medical facility got six inches of water and Weaver told me maintenance would offer their cooperation if the problem could be fixed. I tended to the lot, borrowing their equipment and three inmates. We took the afternoon and redirected the water by filling the interruptions between concrete and blacktop with dirt. With the drains already firmly set, my options were limited. We repaired and unclogged those that were faulty, settling with only a seventy-five percent success ratio. However, this did not sit well with the head of maintenance. My previous work, fixing the cement walkway that his men had ignored, impressed Administration. Now, maintenance just looked incapable because a prisoner located and corrected an error that never should have been. Their anger would only have been intensified if they knew what I would do a month later.

I was attempting a quick cigarette before heading to class on a particularly dismal afternoon. Crossing the lawn, I observed a crew of maintenance men, molding sheets of polyethylene under the surrounding manhole covers. My questions to their intentions were not dignified with a response, and the men continued careless in their work. Essentially, the polyethylene was suffocating the holes, trapping in the often-noticeable odor of feces and garbage. Whoever authorized the work never considered that the garbage and feces that run underground would soon give off a methane gas. Without breathing room, that gas would have no choice, but to filter back into the buildings. The workers did not seem to care and for a short while, I thought, "why should I?"

I left the powerhouse at ten o'clock that same evening. A haze obscured the starlight, magnifying the eerie sight and sound of dancing manhole covers. The polyethylene struggled to prevent the gaseous escape route previously offered, as the covers wrestled for settlement over their circular gaps. I returned to the beach, shaking off the chill of the resonating echo. Before retiring to my cot, I stopped at the bathroom. I was immediately seized by the smell of methane filtering through each vent. Although it was against prison policy to smoke indoors, it was a common occurrence, ignored by many guards. The bathroom was well known as the safest place for the repeated offense. One strike of a match and this methane filled room would have blown the place sky high. My mind quickly painted an all too vivid picture of the consequences.

I assigned one of the inmates to make sure that no one sparked a flame for at least a half an hour. They looked at me like I was a madman as I fled out of there to the closest unlocked janitorial closet. Grabbing a broom, I took my chances against security and ran outside, breaking through the polyethylene with sharp attacks from the broom's handle. I could physically see the contrast of gaseous air as the methane released itself from the punctures. I felt the quivering of my hands as I wiped the perspiration from my rapidly aging brow. The manholes found their serenity. I wondered how long until I could find mine.

The following morning, I paid a visit to my good and reliable associate, Mr. Weaver, telling him about the previous night's events. Weaver was a good guy with good intentions, but too often his hands were tied by bureaucratic paper work. This was one of those incidents.

His office was located in the same building as my cell. It too could have blown up, escalating his concern for the situation only a bit. To avoid a confrontation with maintenance, he asked if I could remove the polyethylene without being detected. He also asked that we deny ever having the conversation.

Weaver made arrangements with the guards on duty that evening, and I grabbed a crew of four men to go outside after curfew. The polyethylene was poured over each hole, forming two separate thick sheets. Since the punctures were already made, we had to peel each layer off. It was time consuming, but successful. We left residual traces of the removed sheets, so when the covers were replaced, it looked as if the polyethylene was still in tact.

Weaver thanked me for the discretion, content that the job went undetected by maintenance. They would find out sooner or later, and hopefully know I was responsible. Maintenance was not the only area that felt my presence. The medical staff was rather displeased when I brought their attention to the false diagnosis of a fellow inmate.

Bobby Rufkins was one of my students, so I had run into him several times in the past. He was a middle-aged man with a mild tone, lacking the confidence and street smarts expected in such a harsh environment. I noticed a slight skin irritation that had progressed into full-blown appled welts, protruding from his clothing. I pulled Bobby aside one day after class, curious to his ailment. He exhibited inflammations on his legs, feet, and chest; none accompanied by the expected itch of a dermatological disorder. I was familiar with skin disease through the medical texts that I read for my own benefit in Allenwood. I read enough to question Bobby's dermatological diagnosis and the cream that was prescribed.

The skin was not irritated externally and the welts seemed to have significant substance behind them, making me believe that it could be something more severe, perhaps blood disease or high cholesterol deposits. My knowledge in no way qualified me for a professional diagnosis, but I did send Bobby back to the infirmary with some questions to ask. After a limited examination, the doctor on duty remained firm in his original diagnosis, criticizing my questions and telling Bobby that I didn't know what I was talking about. I have always found the biggest challenges in life to come from one man's blind doubt. Ironically, Born had typewritten me a similar revelation of his own:

"Recently, I've discovered that when one operates outside the box of conventional thinking and behaving, it causes those who operate within that box to criticize and even question the results gained by the one who has resolved to go against that prevailing pattern. In fact, I believe that a good measure of knowing whether or not one is on the right track comes from the criticism one receives from those who are locked in, therefore, the complainers, criticizers, and haters should be valued and accepted for what they are: good measures of success."

Born's words significantly revealed the maturity of his intellect, but at the same time offered further support in challenging the doctor's diagnosis. I had gone against the doctor's own idea of convention as a prisoner with the knowledge to question. This doctor, attempting to preserve his own pattern, refused to hear any voice but his own. However, his stubbornness involved a human life, one that I refused to sacrifice for the sake of one man's ego.

After carefully noting all of the symptoms, I called Rosemary and relayed the information, asking her, in turn, to call my own doctor at home for as accurate a diagnosis as possible, considering the circumstances. Through my doctor, Rosemary confirmed the following day that a cholesterol problem was likely. The welts on this man's body could have been a result of lethally high cholesterol, that when unattended had turned into fatty deposits. Throughout the patient's time in the infirmary, he had never once been issued a cholesterol test, nor was the infirmary staff eager to do so. Roughly ten other students and I continuously got on the medical staff, insisting upon a cholesterol test for our fellow inmate.

Two weeks later, it was finally issued revealing a dangerous cholesterol count of five hundred and fifty. It was two weeks after the test results, that he was finally prescribed the proper medication. It seemed like everything in Petersburg was becoming a battle.

I had already been in Petersburg for five months and within the Federal Prison Bureau for close to fifteen, when Mr. Weaver pulled me into his office. He told me that my sentence was being reduced by two months for good behavior. I would remain in Petersburg for another month before moving to a community corrections center, a halfway house in Philadelphia. They were sending me back to Pennsylvania, where I would live and work for the remainder of my sentence. I looked forward to leaving. There was no doubt about that, but there was a small part of me that dwelled on what would be left behind. Ironically, this one beaten path led to some good friends, from such different walks of life. My experiences had been great, as were the lessons learned on life, humanity, and myself.

I had two weeks left of my fifth semester teaching. Weaver asked me to stay on for the entire month, teaching half a semester of social studies. I took advantage of the opportunity and began reading up on a subject that I had yet to master. I had taken all my teaching seriously in the past, trying to prepare the students in any way possible for a life outside of prison. I knew that finance and business was not for everyone, that all were not suited for the options I had given. There was a comfort in knowing that each inmate had the choice to take what they wanted from my class and filter it appropriately to their own experiences.

Teaching Social Studies would be different; it would be seen again when taking their General Education Development Test, or GED. Supplying the right answers was essential. It was not a choice for the students, but a necessity. I had never even earned my own GED. I was teaching these students, for the most part successfully, without a high school diploma. With my age and my experience, I no longer deemed a diploma necessary, but for these inmates it could change their lives.

I felt more pressure with my new class approaching, more of an intensity to meet the needs of the whole class. My primary tool for teaching would be the prison-supplied text. In preparation, I implemented my own library research for a more comprehensive understanding. The more I sought reinforcement from my library research, the more I found discrepancies in the text. Dates were wrong and names confused, in addition to a general lack of necessary detail. I brought the discrepancies to the attention of another teacher, a female member of the prison staff. She confirmed the textual errors. Illustrating a genuine concern, she agreed to take the issue up with the Head of Education, assuming he would be more receptive to a staff member than an inmate. I imagined that he could not have been any more abrupt with me, as his message was relayed: "Pileggi should mind his own business." Still, I was satisfied when he recalled all three hundred texts. It was not until class began and the books were reissued that I realized his solution. He had made sure that all pages containing false information were ripped out. Essentially, each of my fifty students received their text, with sixty-seven pages of valuable information missing.

It soon became apparent that the Head of Education cared little for knowledge and plenty for money. The prison's Board of Education earned two thousand five hundred dollars from the government for each GED test administered, regardless of pass or fail. The more inmates failed, the more tests administered, resulting in more money earned by the prison. The Head of Education guaranteed government bonuses by insuring the students remained uneducated. I did everything that I could to defeat his efforts. Since I had previously taken notes on the missing pages, I was able to teach from research alone.

I challenged each student to soak in as much information as possible in the short time allowed, encouraging their progress with a truthful explanation for their tainted texts. Unsuccessfully, I attempted to take a text with me when I left. My intention to expose their education system was probably anticipated, when they searched my few belongings before my departure. Although plenty of inmates were sorry to see me leave, I expected that administration felt a long awaited relief.

At the same time the social studies scam was going on, I ran into larger problems at the powerhouse with my recent transfer to the newly constructed building down the way. I assumed the new powerhouse would be similar to the old, only larger to accommodate the growing inmates and the additional maximum-security prison in progress. Bringing Chico and his ginger snaps with me, I expected nothing different than before, holding the same job responsibility in a more attuned building. With my growing experiences in Petersburg, I should not have been surprised to detect immediate problems.

My sternly built Rock of Gibraltar was replaced by the simplicity of a butler building located next to one of the prison's largest parking lots. Thirty million dollars of combustible equipment resided in this poorly constructed building which failed to meet the required specifications. Signs of cracking were already visible in its concrete foundation while the walls lacked mandatory fire resistance. The gas lines, previously bound through the roof, now excreted natural gas through the walls and downward, directly over open louvers intended to escort fresh air in. Instead, the vents now guided the natural gas back into the building, creating the atmosphere for a potential explosion.

I reported the severity of these hazards to the officers running the plant, creating a fear among them. I had only two weeks left at Petersburg. These men were required by a weekly paycheck to remain much longer. The majority seemed to feel helpless against the already completed building and agreed that whoever approved the construction was most likely paid off. In an attempt to shave costs, that person had also shaved the safety of the facility. I did not know if I was looking for a solution or just advice, but either way I reported the problem to Weaver, knowing it was not his department. Weaver failed to make his usual excuse of bureaucratic red tape. Refusing to tiptoe around such severity, he immediately ordered an investigation of the problem. As a precaution, I surrendered my home phone and address at his request, anticipating a desired testimony at future legal proceedings. It was my understanding that the investigation would continue past my release from Petersburg. With my departure approaching, I handed over the position to a reliable replacement, Jimmy Clarke. Jimmy was another inmate, formally a federally employed engineer, serving time on drummed up charges regarding government contracts. I relinquished my duties and Chico to his care.

I was discharged at R&D just before noon on March 12, 2001, gladly relinquishing my prison uniform for the comfort of street clothes. After close to sixteen months in prison, Petersburg had granted my long awaited released, placing me in the temporary custody of my two sons. Ted and Jim had driven to Virginia the night before, sharing a restful night's sleep in a local hotel room, in preparation for the long day to follow. My sentence was not yet complete. The boys were merely the middlemen, bound by law to deliver me directly to 325 North Broad Street in Philadelphia, a privately owned community corrections center, under contract and monitored by the Federal Bureau of Prisons.

My release from prison resembled a common portrayal in the movies. Two guards escorted me by foot the length of the prison's extended driveway. Our destination was the gated exit ahead, locked and secured with overhead ringlets of barbed wire. My anticipation rose with the gate's proximity, as my boys lingered anxiously on the opposite side. Both of my boys, one past and one just reaching thirty years old, looked like children again. They reminded me of a business trip a long time ago, when I had returned to their innocent faces in wait of Daddy's gifts. Seeing them like this softened the very core of my soul, generating old forgotten sensations.

The five-hour drive, from Virginia to Pennsylvania, was a phenomenon not likely to be described. I was coming forth from a dark den into the blessed light and air. I felt as if I had been confined to a box for sixteen months and, at last, I was able to stretch my legs. The unbound tone of freedom surrounded me, in the voices of my sons, in the perfume of highway wind, in the flavor of civilization, and in the image of nature's splendid dyes. My senses were exhausted, making up for lost time.

The halfway house did not scare me. For the remaining three months of my sentence, I would reside there, working in the community while preparing for my final release. My probation officer had warned me of what to expect, and it was not much. After the places that I have been, I did not amuse myself with expectations. The time remaining was only a drop in the bucket. It was one step closer to my former life revived.

Chapter 14

THE HALFWAY HOUSE

My sons delivered me to my new community residence on Broad Street shortly after five. Externally, the corrections center blended with the series of old Philly style red brick structures. Internally, the speckled asphalt tiled floors illuminated the cold drear of its dirty white washed walls. The building resembled a boarding house, with three stories of dorm-like rooms. To accommodate its average of a hundred and eighty residents, three to five men or women were assigned per room.

Unlike most halfway houses, it was gender mixed, upholding the segregation of sexes through floors. My floor was the second, swarming with drug or alcohol dependents, seeking outside rehabilitation before seeking employment. Overcrowding was encouraged since the center received a daily government reimbursement of one hundred and fifteen dollars per inmate. After reviewing the dilapidated decor, I found myself missing

Petersburg. Petersburg was a dark dirty hole, but it had the integrity to never claim different.

The halfway house was intended to be a semblance of normality. Rather, it reflected the nature of the beast in its stifling heat, immobile elevators, soiled facilities, and cobwebbed corners. Administration ran the place similarly strict to the prison, with pill calls, meal times, and regular counts. However, at night, I noticed a leniency in the recreation room downstairs, where both genders socialized. With pornography on the television, the gender barrier dissolved as male hands invaded the welcoming mini skirts of female residents. I witnessed this only once when a roommate confirmed that it was a regular occurrence. It was then that I realized a difference between the inmates in prison and the residents at this particular center. In prison, I found some good men with poor judgment. The center, at this time, lacked any characters similar. I opted not to socialize, and instead reviewed letters sent from Born and Moses, content in the confinement of my room.

Born first sent a letter of thanks, saying that through my example he has seen what he could become by staying "humble, truthful, and hungry." He wrote, "Tom, you and I both know that it was not by chance that our paths crossed. It was through a bigger plan. I have learned from you to value quality over quantity, and the time we did share was rewarding and encouraging." It made me feel good. I was better off than those guys, and I knew it. I had been given better opportunities from the start and was blessed with the knowledge to take advantage of them. In the past, Born was the kind of man that I would have stayed away from. It was through a bigger plan that our paths crossed, and Born was not the only one feeling its reward.

Moses' letter was more personal, referring to us as a team and reflecting the depth of our closeness by saying, "the fabric of which we have built our friendship is of the best material." After he had reviewed the obstacles and hurdles survived on my journey, he apologized for "selfishly" not wanting to accept the reality of my release. Moses added that to his joy was the knowledge that I would be "going to a better environment," or at least a place where I "will receive the proper medical attention." We were both disillusioned in believing my new environment would be better.

I did not want to dishearten him with the truth. Instead, I merely wrote a letter supporting his own journey's conclusion: "To Buckwheat, every dream takes time to grow. From small beginnings come great things. You are the famous Buckwheat and no one can take that from you." I would have rather stayed at Petersburg, where I could teach and perhaps be of some worth. At Petersburg, I felt that I could make a difference, that I could affect some lives for the better. At the halfway house, my first two weeks were idle, waiting for my working papers to be approved.

In Petersburg, my request for employment at Colonial Mortgage had been approved, allowing me to work in an environment with which I was familiar. Colonial Mortgage was a successful financial company in business for over eighty years. It was also conveniently located in one of my developments, offering close proximity to my own office. Once arriving at the halfway house, they denied my request, excusing the company as too similar to my own. Within days, my Case Manager, Mr. Keller, was sent a letter from a restaurant owner, who coincidentally occupied the store space next to Colonial. The owner had offered to employ me as kitchen manager of his seafood restaurant. Keller agreed and I was offered a two hundred dollar weekly salary for the three months of mandatory employment. I had Rosemary ask the owner to keep my salary low. I did not need the money and the halfway house would take twenty five percent of the gross wages earned.

Someone was benefiting royally at the community correction center and it was not its residents. As mentioned earlier, the center was reimbursed one hundred and fifteen dollars a day for each resident, in addition to confiscating twenty-five percent of gross earnings. Phone calls from the halfway house were five dollars for the first minute alone. When Rosemary received a phone bill for fifteen hundred dollars, she filed a complaint with the center. They knocked off a thousand dollars without any question. It seemed like one large racket, with money as the primary motivation for business.

Each newly assigned resident was required a mandatory physical examination from the center's own appointed doctor. I refused, insisting upon my own doctor in Abington, only a short distance away. I was told that it would be impossible, and besides their doctor would cost me nothing. Perhaps not, but it was costing the taxpayers. The government was charged a hundred and twenty dollars for each visit to their doctor. I would need over twenty appointments with a variety of specialists, to get myself into the same health enjoyed before prison. My stubbornness paid off and soon the administration amended their policy, approving visits to the doctor of my choice. The center was still entitled to a hundred dollars of government money every evening when I was required to urinate in a cup for drug testing.

Each trip from the halfway house was stringently monitored, whether for a doctor's appointment or to go to work. I checked in by phone at my arrival and again directly before departing. During the day, my case manager would visit the restaurant unannounced, ensuring the veracity of my employment. Although Moses had shared some of his restaurant insight, I do not believe I made a very good kitchen manager. I did, however, save the owner several thousands of dollars in constructing a new restaurant. My new career certainly was not a future option, but I was thankful for the opportunity and the decent meals, a rarity since Rochester.

For thirty-five days, I resided at the halfway house, leaving at eight each weekday morning for work and making sure to return by seven in the evening. On the weekends, I acquired a pass to attend church. Otherwise, I just read in my room or roamed the scanty grounds. On April 17, I was no longer required to reside in the community corrections center. I continued working in the restaurant, giving them my twenty-five percent, but left from and returned to my home. Once home, the hours of employment decreased to only the required minimum. The center would still receive their government compensation for another two months, until the formal end of my sentence. They were happy to have the open bed, which meant more government money.

I checked in regularly, as they checked on me with phone calls in the middle of the night and unexpected visits during the day. It worked for me. I could not complain because I was home at last. Everything in life seemed so much more spectacular than when I left. My entire world took on a newly enlightened air of brilliance, as if civilization intensified overnight in both color and pleasure for my delight alone.

At my own dinner table, I enjoyed hot healthy meals, cooked in the oven and basking in flavor. I had water pressure in my private shower. Hell, I had toilet seats! My house appeared larger and Liz softer. Every word from her voice was like a mastered symphony, oozing with the depth of emotion and bringing me to the brink of tears. I could hear the cars pass on the road and they sang like birds in the nearby sanctuary. I could run out my door and dance in my pajamas. I had pajamas and they were clean and smelled so very fresh. Life! Life! Life! How I enjoyed every waking moment! I reveled in it for as long as I could.

Chapter 15

DIRT ROADS

My glory lasted as long as the thoughtless mind allowed. As a thinking man, the novelty wore off with surfacing questions. Why was I blindly enjoying this rebirth of basic existence? Simple. Because I had been denied it for so long. What was the source of this denial? That was a question for which I had no reply. My search for the answer led to a rising anger, more like an irritation that had been buried within the routine of prison survival.

I did not regret my time in prison. Experience is a teacher indeed, and I appreciated the nineteen-months of education. My hostility dwelled not in the awareness of a different world, but in the individuals, whom wrongly stole my freedom and with it my reputation and good name. In the eyes of many, I was now an ex-convict, a criminal released from the Federal Bureau of Prisons. I was subjected to whispering behind my back and jokes at my expense. The people who did not know me were now open to doubt me. My name and my integrity, including everything that I had worked for in life, no longer belonged to me, the real me. They belonged to Tom Pileggi, the man convicted of insider trading.

Two years after the verdict, it was still so unfathomable. How does this happen? How can the impossible become reality? Reader, imagine your own life, your own good deeds, and your own good nature. Now, imagine it all being corrupted with the false accusations of others. Imagine how you would attempt to save your own business and the jobs of your co-workers. Now, imagine being rewarded with almost two years void of freedom and family. I had attempted to save a bank and the two hundred and sixty jobs that came with it. I had attempted to establish the largest charitable organization in Philadelphia. Somewhere, the people and events involved in the two unavoidable failures had intertwined, resulting in a legal defense of my values and actions.

My family tells me that their faith and my own is enough. We know that I am innocent and anyone familiar with me will believe it as well. But, for me, it is not enough. I will not shy away from the truth, waving a white flag of surrender. Since my release, friends have directed me to seek pardon, but I refuse. There is no pardon for innocence, only guilt. Instead, I seek a different means for justice, a literary means. I extend my voice upon paper, sacrificing my soul and my memories, for an unobstructed proclamation of truth. It is a truth not found in a political campaign, or in prosecutor misconduct, or even in deals with the government. It is a truth found within my heart and my spirit.

My battle has only begun, and I will not concede until my record expunged and my name cleared. At best, I can hope to regain my dignity and reputation. However, there is no compensation for the lost time or the missing sense of normality. Normal is a term with which I am no longer familiar. The initial reality of that angered me on a daily basis. I was angry with myself for getting caught in such an elaborate trap. I was angry with the individuals and organizations that guaranteed my nineteen-month suspension of life. Above all, I was angry that my efforts to pick up where I left off were in vain. Nothing would again return to "normal."

After my release from prison, Liz was a different woman, as loving and faithful as ever, but more independent. I, by no means, returned to her the same man and she would never fully understand why. I had sheltered Liz along the way, telling her only what I thought she could handle. I had deprived her of my experience and the strength she had displayed over the years. My penance was a strained relationship. How could I explain my lost desire for business; my sleepless days revitalizing the garden; and my tendency to remain confined to only thirty inches of our king size bed? I could not detail prison's effect because I was not sure of it myself. I returned believing myself to be the same man, and in many respects I was. However, gradually, I would identify little changes, sometimes insignificant and sometimes not. Liz and I survived it, as I knew we would. The struggles come and go, but the love remains.

Rosemary kept me abreast of business through my daily prison calls. I returned to the office for business as usual, only to find my building passion had faded. Rosemary and my son Jim successfully maintained both businesses in my absence. First Cheltenham Financial Corp. flourished under Rosemary's sharp eye and good judgment. Before prison, I sold Krista's Kastle, replenishing the money lost in my trial. Doing so had freed up my finances, giving Rosemary the leeway needed as power of attorney. Over the past two years, while I was preoccupied with the trial and then prison, Rosemary continued to approve mortgages and authorize loans.

With her shared dedication to the business, First Cheltenham earned its value as a reputable mortgage company, servicing the community in its six years of business.

I returned with First Cheltenham Financial Corporation as my primary focus. The continuing development of First Cheltenham replenished my hopes of one day reviving a people's bank, made for and by the people. Perhaps naively, I still believed that I would one day be reunited with the remaining Cheltenham employees. With several Cheltenham employees already lost, I resolved to offer similar opportunities to their children.

Josephine Cotignola died on November 11, 2000, while I was in Petersburg, only three months after her original cancer diagnosis. She was only fifty-three years old. When I had first returned home, I landscaped her gravesite for six hours. Mildred Sweeney had died after a brief illness. I had been denied a pass for both funerals, along with several others. First Cheltenham appeared to be my closest means of regaining what was lost. It represented my faith in the people, and more importantly, my faith in the good guy. I concentrated on First Cheltenham as my last grapple for justice, my final attempt to make things right. Consequently, my building career seemed to pale in comparison.

While in prison, Tom Pileggi and Associates generated most of its profits through monthly rents on the properties owned. Skillfully trained in the business, Jim took on minor projects here and there, while utilizing his marketing degree in the office. I returned to only a few projects, waiting in the wings. After reviewing the paperwork and attempting to take them up, I resolved to hand over all building responsibilities to Jim. Building was not the same. Something had been lost either in myself or in the business—perhaps, in both. In my youth, I was one of the biggest builders in the Bucks County area. At fifty-six years old, I was the smallest and thankful to escape the force of its clenching grip. I supposed, at the time, that I had lost my building edge. In actuality, I had gained a realization of my mortality. This was it, only one life, and building had monopolized so many of its years. I wanted to seize this life, before it seized me. Time and experience were passing too quickly.

I was attempting to slow things down, to decelerate my foothold on life, while the people around me zoomed past. I began to notice an intensifying need for speed, acceleration on the world and its daily procedures. It existed, no doubt, before prison, when I too was caught up in the haste. People were driving their expensive fast cars, racing to get nowhere in a hurry. They stormed by in the supermarket, the gas station, or the fast food restaurant. Aware of no one but themselves, they rushed to be someplace else. Where? When was it time to appreciate the present, rather than always looking toward the future? Were they chasing the constant hand of Father Time? Or, were they fleeing the random shadow of death's wings?

I no longer fear death. I will never hunt it, yet I refuse to cower in its presence. Life has granted me a worthy spell, treasured with a variety of experience and accomplishment. For me, death is the beginning of a new life. It is the snake shedding its skin in preparation of the changing season. It is a path yet to be explored or a new road to travel. Perhaps, it would be a more simplistic road, a dirt road, leading to a porch light comfort we spend our lives searching to find.

I no longer fear death; but while alive, I will delight in life. Not exploring the Internet, where the world is at my fingertips, while my neighbor is beyond reach. Not driving a sports car, when the 120,000 miles on my Ford gets me where I need to go. Not residing in an elaborate mansion, where only a single bedroom is needed. Not pecking at a laptop computer, when my loose-leaf binder does not need charging. I will enjoy life for what it is and not what it was or what it could be. I will enjoy life for its simplicity and not for its complications.

Somewhere along the line, simplicity was lost, taking with it our values. Materialism seems to have taken its place. Success is increasingly measured by money, rather than achievements, nationally encouraged by overseas corporate expansion. Employees are being downsized, requiring maximum effort for minimum pay. Consequently, family income has replaced family values. Children are abandoned to the care of strangers, as careers are worshiped more than kids. As a nation, we are encouraged to emphasize the dollar's value, as it loses worth in a steady decline of buying power.

Prices increase, but salaries do not, rendering it more difficult to achieve the national definition of success. For household expenditures comparable to twenty-five years ago, a modern family needs to gross one hundred and twenty five thousand dollars a year in income, twice the national average. If I had held onto three hundred of my original properties, today they would value more than all three thousand in my building career. Real estate is increasingly overvalued, requiring the consumer to fuel investments several times beyond the product's original worth.

Financial agencies play the percentages, making a profit off the services that, in reality, we provide. Banks offer a minimal percent on the money we supply, averaging four percent on CD's, and even less on the money loaned through general savings. That same money is redistributed in the average loan, suffering an increased percentile and earning the bank over a hundred percent profit on our original investment. Credit card companies play a similar game, earning fourteen to eighteen percent on the annual percentage rate. Their rates are worse than loan sharks, producing three times the profit on their original investment scale. Yet, the world increasingly relies on plastic, guaranteeing luxury outside of their means.

We look to the government for assistance and find only an escalation of taxes, to the point that a single dollar passed four times in a thirty percent tax bracket turns into $1.20 in tax, taxing thirty cents on the same dollar each time it changes hands. In a twenty percent tax bracket, the dollar is passed five times to earn its own value. We spend the money left after taxes, subjecting ourselves to a purchasing tax on the product or service. Please understand that I am not against taxes, nor am I ignorant of their value. Taxes are essential for our country and I pay them gladly. My attempt is not to belittle the system of taxation, but rather to control it.

This issue of taxes and national economic growth is not new to me. It is one that I have considered and discussed openly since the early eighties, when I had first brought my concerns to the attention of President Ronald Reagan and members of the Senate. I had the rare opportunity to correspond with the former President on several occasions. More often than not, our correspondences dealt with proposed solutions in erasing the national deficit.

As a youth, I found opportunities had always been present. With proper timing, a little luck, and a lot of hard work, I made the most of those opportunities. Today, the opportunities are still there, but much harder to uncover. For the sake of the younger generation, I had begun my correspondences with the intent of reinstating the United States as the land of opportunity.

In 1983, I had written to fifty Senators with one comprehensive solution. Of the fifty, twenty-five wrote back, extending thanks for my consideration and praises for my efforts. However, it was evident that only two of the Senators fully understood my program, one going so far as to extend a Washington invitation.

My program, based on a simple mathematical equation, had been proposed as a solution to the national debt without raising taxes. Although outdated by numbers today, my intentions remain unaltered. At the time, four hundred and fifty billion dollars had been spent in tax shelters every year, which our government never saw. By turning the national debt into a vast tax shelter on a 2 for 1 basis, every dollar going in would have been rendered as two dollars in tax savings. The social and corporate classes would have been eligible for the program on a one to three year basis, depending on their individual needs. In other words, instead of buying tax shelters, we would all buy a piece of the debt in exchange for tax breaks.

Within eight months, the government could have collected enough money to pay off the debt and balance the budget at the same time. With the debt paid off, the government would have saved billions of dollars in unemployment compensation, returning people to work and therefore, increasing tax revenue. Interest rates would fall, and the dollar would be restored to its original value. It would have been the birth of a strong new economy, nurtured by its country's citizens. Although simply put for the sake of brevity, it was my master financial plan, never reaching further than the rare open-minded politician.

I have a psychological plan as well, much less complex. The United States needs to slow down. Society is going too fast, and eventually we will crash. We need to take a deep breath and reassess where our newly found ideals will lead. A return to simplicity and family values would invigorate the simpler pleasures of life so often missed. The moon's mysterious hue enlivening dense wooded trees; the smell of honeysuckles enveloping a ripe summer afternoon; a star shooting across the elaborately lit sky—these are the things that matter. These are the living jewels, not money or man-made material. The most valuable possession in life is the intangible freedom to feel and think. On that, there could never be a price tag. Money should be no man's master, but rather his servant to do good deeds.

I have followed that philosophy my entire life, beginning with minor donations to Saint James church at the age of six. As a child and in the most impoverished times, my parents had remained faithful to their charitable values. With sparing fancies of our own, my siblings and I had been reminded that others had less. I remembered this with every penny earned, sharing each development profit with worthy organizations. As my financial success increased, I made a conscious decision to increase contributions and involvement, donating a plethora of time and money to various local charities over the years.

In April of 1992, I ceremoniously received the Inter-Faith award for devotion and humanitarian services. The American/Israeli Red Cross honored me as their recipient in recognition of humanitarian work and philanthropic endeavors with people of all races. Only one month later, Montgomery County had offered a similar recognition. The same year, the Pennsylvania Senate acknowledged my outstanding record of service and leadership in keeping with the highest ideals of the Commonwealth. I never donated for the accreditation, but rather for the consideration of those less fortunate, of those offered less chances. I believe in people and the power of the human spirit. My donations had been viewed as an extension of that spirit, an extension of a world beyond my bedroom window.

I always tried to keep my charities and sympathies broad, supporting the less fortunate overseas, as well as at home. *Seeds of Peace* seemed an untraditional charity when first introduced to me years ago by another builder and good friend. Today, its significance is magnified, as is its support. *Seeds of Peace* is a nonprofit, nonpolitical organization that helps teenagers from regions of conflict learn the skills of making peace. A yearly camp in the woods of Maine offers a safe and supportive environment where the children can express their views. At the same time, they are educated in listening, communication, and other conflict resolution techniques that allow them to develop empathy for one another. Ideally, it equips the next generation with the capabilities to dissolve the ongoing cycles of violence. The kids become friends despite nationality and politics, allowing them the future potential to straighten out the problems created by the generations before. The more that I attend fundraising functions, the more that I believe in their cause.

In my earlier years, I focused on the more conventional charities, the charities that dealt primarily with money and aid, rather than education. The Variety Club in Philadelphia had become the most favorable, at the start of my business career. Variety raises essential funds for the care and support of disadvantaged, physically challenged, sick and needy children around the world. Their creed proudly states, "No one stands taller than when helping a child." The money donated in Philadelphia stays in the community, supporting the programs and facilities that benefit the children in and around that area. Liz and I believed in Variety. We believed in giving other children the same opportunities as our own.

The author (right) with Joan Rivers and Donnie Epstein,
President of Variety Club, in 1985.

Our local *Channel 6* appeared to be one of *Variety's* greatest sponsors, offering frequent airtime. I supported them, assuming their airtime donations a reflection of community generosity. Years later, I had found that *Channel 6* had been charging the organization for the service and exposure, dismissing charity for business as usual. I began to question where else my donations were being squandered. Who else was getting paid and how much were the children benefiting from that pay? As a matter of fact, a large percentage of all contributions had gone to the hefty salaries of administration. For a nonprofit organization, some of their employees were profiting quite well. I have noticed this with many other charities as well, cautioning my donations with the means of distribution.

Just before prison, I was ironically introduced to a different form of charity, one in which this same misdistribution of funds had become apparent. After the trial, I took measures to send fruit baskets to the many individuals involved with the case. Joan Leiby, as head of the probation department, had been one of the recipients. As a government employee, she sent a letter of thanks, telling me that she was unable to accept the generous offer. She took it upon herself to donate the basket to the Douglas House, a community corrections center in Philadelphia for mentally challenged inmates released from prison.

I never intended on donating to such a cause, nor had I realized that such a place existed. After receiving her letter, I called Leiby directly to get more information on this halfway house. Mentally challenged inmates were and are an ongoing concern for both the state and federal government. In this imperfect world, many of these individuals receive prison confinement in place of psychological treatment. Often, poorly adjusted to their prison environment, they repeatedly act out, relinquishing the chance at early release under probationary supervision. Consequently, their entire sentence, including probation, has been served in full at the time of their release. Unsupervised, they leave prison as socially misplaced as when they arrived, increasing the likelihood of a future offense.

The Douglas House offers a rare community service that should be viewed as a necessity. It serves as a transitional stage in which the mentally challenged criminal can gradually be reintroduced and readjusted to society. Ms. Leiby offered the brief history of the center and its benefits, convincing me of the organization's value. I solicited the necessary information to send a monetary donation and promised to visit the Douglas House at my convenience.

Several months before my own prison sentence, I found the opportunity to meet Bob Kurtz, the director of the Douglas House, on his own grounds. During our meeting, Bob displayed the utmost sincerity in achieving the center's goals. Today, I can say from experience that Bob Kurtz is one of the most honest and warmhearted men employed through the system. Bob gave me a tour of the decaying building, excusing its appearance to a lack of financial resources. He told me of his own problems with bureaucratic red tape, and the increasing obstacles ignored by the center's corporate owners. I left the Douglas House moved by Bob's dedication, and showed it by writing the Douglas House a check, to be used at Bob's discretion.

Bob called me weeks later, extending an invitation to witness the rewards of my donation. Just previously, I received a thank you letter from the parent company in response to my first contribution. I accepted Bob's invitation, intending to first visit the parent company's headquarters in Philadelphia. I arrived at North Western Human Services, anticipating a discussion on the Douglas House's problems. I had planned on offering some financial assistance to find solutions. Upon entering North Western, I was struck by its pristine interior, as I crossed the marbled lobby floors that shone freshly polished beneath the cathedral chandelier lit ceiling. With the distinct recollection of their fading subsidiary, I left, unfulfilling my goal. I decided that all future donations be placed in Bob's prudence.

I visited the Douglas House as planned, and told Bob of my future intentions. During our discussion of greed's controlling hand, he expressed the desperate need for a minibus, which the corporation had refused for years to allow in the budget. The next week, I visited my local Ford dealer, purchasing a fifteen-passenger bus. I took some time, lettering it myself with the Douglas House name, and donated it directly to Bob, avoiding corporate interference.

I continued to correspond with Bob, making small donations here and there, until my own sentencing had begun. At my request, Rosemary maintained relations, offering assistance, food, or money whenever needed. While in Rochester, Joan Leiby sent me a letter, partially on Bob's behalf. She thanked me again for all of my contributions, saying, "They [The Douglas House] are glad to receive what they have from you, but they would prefer to know that you're fine, even if you can't visit." Before I replied, I called Rosemary, instructing her to make another donation.

Bob was one of the good guys, one of the Westricks and the Guises, rarely found in the system. He never asked me for anything, but he humbly accepted whatever I could offer. Financially, Bob is by no means wealthy. His paycheck forbids it, but he is rich. He is rich in compassion and nature, illustrating it in the daily service that he provides. Bob's prosperity is measured not in the money he makes, but in the pride he takes. It was a similar pride that allowed Dr. Westrick to avoid government mandatory retirement at the age of sixty-five. Equally proud, Guise earned the title of Lieutenant and the respect of his men. I hoped that one day, Bob would secure a community corrections center of his own, one in which profit came secondary to people.

Chapter 16

THE GARDEN

My experiences with the not-so-good guys had taken their toll. I never particularly realized until pointed out by others, that I was less social. I reported to the office regularly, restricting myself to only a few hours a day. I still had my visitors and made my visits, taking care of necessary business and maintaining worthy friendships. However, I was more withdrawn, less likely to instigate conversation or make acquaintances beyond the old. There was no doubt to my increased caution, resulting from the duality of human nature observed. Although the lesson was harsh, I learned that people, mankind in general, were not always as they appeared. I would not say that I was a cynic, more a realist. In this reality, I was happier being alone. I found myself dedicating most time to the nurturing of my gardens, giving in to its wild whims with perfect abandon.

As the gardener's son, I had always taken interest in my yard, throwing a hospitable smile over its manicured gardens. I returned home with the taste of prison still lingering on my tongue, and found my yard to parallel my previous year. The grass blades, although freshly mowed, flaunted their browned split tips; and the bushes once so carefully pruned had grown in indignant lack of proportion. My aristocratic flowers had lost their regal air to the frequent begging of water and sunlight. In the past, I had escaped to the gardens, allowing my breath to mingle with the busy fragrance that floated through the air. Revisiting my yard, after such time passed, I no longer sensed their vitality to the scene. I breathed the same air, finding only an atmosphere of Sorrow.

I took to my gardens, proving to Sorrow that he could not reach me there. Revitalizing the grounds with the same intensity of my past career, I constructed a fairytale landscape. Beginning gradually, I weeded and pruned on the weekends. Soon, I was taking time off work to browse my brother's nursery. I restored life when I could, and plucked the last bit of existence when I could not. I dug, hoed, and weeded, grazing my fingers through the heavy earth, to refresh myself with any nature and simplicity that may be remaining. Gold touched tiki torches and Christmas lighted trees allowed me to continue working despite the hour. At Liz's aggravation, I spent many sleepless nights, leaving the dinner table for the gardens and not returning until breakfast the following morning. It was an obsession to her, but therapy for me. Gradually, every portion of soil was peopled with plants, flowers, ornaments or fountains.

Now, turns of the yard are thematically arranged particular to each grandchild, marked by varying sized cement statues of childlike resemblance. One frozen likeness rests centrally located at the rear of the house. Positioned beneath a rose-laced trellis, it peaks four feet high from encircling bloom, at the heart of a sculptured ring of shrubbery. The haven is set in white stone, paved in its bed with mosaic colored marbles.

Another statue, much smaller in size, stands on top a golden birdbath, cuddling two young children beneath a similarly colored umbrella. Located at the yard's iron gated entrance, the bath's tranquil waters sparkle with sunbeams, pronouncing the children's persistent cheer. And yet, two other life-sized reproductions guard the home's red-bricked walkway among a well-selected assortment of blossomed gems, basking in the sun.

Hand-painted wagon trains, pinwheels, wishing wells and windmills, adorn the remaining elaborately dressed lawn. Numerous chimes sing in the summer breeze, entertaining ceramic animals strategically placed within the wild-flowering azaleas, impatiens, geraniums, petunias, and lilies. A degree of careful labor and a plenitude of moisture nourishes the gigantic leaves and the zenith of gorgeously magnificent blossoms that exist today. They are wild; yet somehow maintain a gentle grace. Each flower differs amongst itself, in its perfumed spirit and its particular lustered jewels.

Round-slated footsteps over a flower rimmed white stone walkway bridge the lawn to the focal point of the front yard. It is a fourteen by fourteen foot solar-lit gazebo, contoured with hanging floral baskets. Opposite its painted pebble entrance, lay the immortal spirit of a lively fountain, ornamented with angels to exaggerate the slight agitation of its upward gush. To the right of the fountain, at the driveway's border, a quite unique statue resides, breaking the heavenly pattern of my landscape.

The statue was originally designed to resemble Buddha, but with some paints and props, it is now the likeness of Ed Rendell. The plump face is capped with slick black hair, while a pair of reading glasses rests across its flat, wide nose. The protruding belly and accompanying upper body is coated in yellow and black stripes, suggesting stereotypical prison garb. Across the chest, a plate is secured with the name of Ed Rendell, Allenwood Prison, and a bogus prison identification number. The statue's hands rise joyfully over its head, shackled in chains. From the lower arm, a leash is attached to an appropriate pet, a cold-blooded amphibian, flipping out its tongue to capture prey. The oversized and over exaggerated concrete bullfrog possesses wide beady eyes and a conniving smile upon its rough, wart covered skin. A lawn light rises to its side, so that the portrait can be appreciated through the night.

I watch the Buddha and his bullfrog, remembering Rendell and his start as District Attorney. A Catholic priest and dear friend of mine had told me a joke many years ago, that I am just beginning to fully comprehend.

The Pope dies and goes to Heaven, where he meets Saint Peter waiting at the gates. Naturally, Saint Peter opens the gates, welcoming His Eminence with a nice horse, a sturdy cow, a Volkswagen, and a lovely two-bedroom home with a nicely manicured lawn, only six blocks from the beach. The Pope, quite pleased, thanks Saint Peter and shows his appreciation.

The following day, an elderly man in his late 70's, dies and again, Saint Peter meets him at the gates. Saint Peter welcomes him with a mansion on the ocean, a Rolls Royce, an Olympic-size pool, two tennis courts, and a fully staffed yacht. Witnessing such good fortune being bestowed on the elderly man, the Pope asks Saint Peter, "St. Peter," the Pope said, "please realize that I am not complaining. I'm very thrilled with all that you've given me. Yet, I can't help but question why this other fellow has earned such a large estate."

"I understand, Your Eminence," St. Peter replied. "But, you have to realize that this is the first time ever that a lawyer has made it into Heaven."

I was searching for my own traces of Heaven. Although I had found solace in the gardens, my Buddha reminded me of a disruptive peace of mind and a resentment not easily shaken. The yard work was indeed therapeutic, distracting me with its fairytale design. It was my temporary escape from the people and past situations that have stirred my confidence in mankind. I had been postponing the inevitable, a return to reality. Within the gardens, I had control. I created results complimentary to my expectations. My life had not been as easy.

We all have expectations, some easy to achieve while others a struggle to realize. Never in my wildest dreams or my frenzied nightmares, would I have expected to go to prison. Never, could I have expected to make friends like Born and Moses, or to establish First Cheltenham Financial, or to write my autobiography. If there is one thing that I have learned, it is that life does not always meet our expectations. And often, we find the most unexpected opportunities in our most feared circumstances. Now, I keep up my gardens in moderation, after finding a balance between reality and fantasy.

My reality has returned me to the building business, on a part-time basis. I limit myself to the occasional home, without the old time thrill. First Cheltenham Financial Corporation continues to expand with increasing investments, allowing me to anticipate bank status in the next three years. When the opportunity is introduced, I explore various legal options at clearing my name. Time with my family and friends has increased with the awareness of time's limits.

Through my experiences, I have made the transition from my former, simpler sphere of life to a world more abundant and knowing. I recognize that no matter how much one resolves to stick with the main path of life, bypaths are introduced that cannot be easily withstood. My protection is now my prudence and conscientious. I remind myself of the advantages to blatantly saying, "NO." Remaining cautious of the weaknesses that accompany good nature, I attempt to choose my experiences, before they choose me.

Today, I sit at my desk, considering various choices for publication. Staring at Frankie's picture across the way, I remember our times together. How pleased he would be at my life's journey and its diversity of experience.